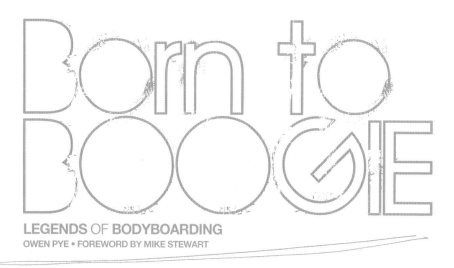

# Born to BOOGIE

## LEGENDS OF BODYBOARDING

OWEN PYE • FOREWORD BY MIKE STEWART

**Published by Orca Publications**
Berry Road Studios
Berry Road
Newquay
Cornwall
TR7 1AT
United Kingdom
(+44) 01637 878074
www.threesixtymag.co.uk
www.orcasurf.co.uk

EDITOR: **MIKE SEARLE**
EDITORIAL CONSULTANT: **ROB BARBER**
DESIGN: **DAVID ALCOCK, MIKE SEARLE**
DISTRIBUTION CONSULTANT: **CHRIS POWER**

**PHOTOGRAPHERS:** Sacha Specker, Mike Searle, Brian Bielmann, Tom Boyle, Chris Power, Scott Winer, Tim Jones, Chris Stroh, Peto, Tungsten, Phil Gallagher.

ISBN: 978-0-9567893-2-7

PRINTED AND BOUND: **GREAT WALL PRINTING, HONG KONG**

**Thank you to everyone who has made this book possible,** principally publisher Mike Searle for his unwavering patience, and associates Rob Barber and Chris Power for their honesty and feedback; to every interviewee for opening up their lives, memories and remarkable stories (not to mention for giving hundreds of hours to my coffee-fuelled questioning); to all contributors and photographers who have helped provide such a stunning collection of images throughout the book (a special thanks to Sacha Specker for offering his amazing library of images to us); to my loving parents, family and girlfriend Nikky for their support and tolerance during the year, and to all those people and institutions who have given their time to help bring this story to print – it is long overdue.

This book is dedicated to all the bodyboarders who have made this sport what it is. *– Owen Pye*

Brian Wise drops into a bomb
at the 2012 IBA Pipeline Pro.

# Contents

Jack 'Da Ripper' Lindholm drives hard
off the bottom with characteristic power.

# Intro

The definiation of style. Spencer Skipper poised and perfect, North Shore, mid 1990s.

**B**odyboarding, the art of riding waves prone on some form of water craft, is not new. For thousands of years Pacific Islanders slid across ocean swells lying down, immersed in the simple pleasure of letting a pulse of energy move them to shore across a breaking wave. From honed *paipo* boards in Hawaii to modest bundles of reeds in Rapa Nui, 18th Century European explorers recounted tales of primal bodyboarding in

*From honed paipo boards in Hawaii to modest bundles of reeds in Rapa Nui, 18th Century European explorers recounted tales of primal bodyboarding in Tahiti, New Zealand, the Marquesas Islands, and throughout Melanesia, Micronesia and Western Polynesia.*

Tahiti, New Zealand, the Marquesas Islands, and throughout Melanesia, Micronesia and Western Polynesia.

Over the next couple of hundred years however it was the evolution of stand-up surfing which rose to the fore in social consciousness, as humble bodyboarding took a back seat. Step forward Tom Morey, who, in 1971, reintroduced the ancient art to the masses with his phenomenon: the Boogie Board. Over the next four decades the sport took off, developing its own industry, companies, competitions, tours, sponsorships, markets and media, attracting an estimated six million participants around the world. Bodyboarding had woken from its slumber, and was here to stay.

My introduction to the sport began in 1996 at Praa Sands shorey on the south coast of Cornwall, UK. I had just started secondary school, and my new friends were keen to get me in the winter waves. Sporting a 3/2mm shortie wetsuit in the 6C (43F) degree water on a grey February afternoon, I was pushed into my first wave on a pink Styrofoam board lent to me by my friend's younger sister. The surf was all of 1ft and dumped me onto the sand, but I was instantly hooked, and splashed my way back out to try again. I eventually exited the water a worrying shade of blue and shivering uncontrollably, but I'd been bitten by the bug, and though I didn't know it at the time, it would change my entire life path.

Bodyboarding has introduced me to new places, new cultures and new people. With it I've travelled the world, discovered new waves, witnessed incredible nature and experienced beautiful and humbling moments that will stay with me for life... it helped shape everything. No matter where I went I was endlessly searching coastlines, looking for setups, wondering about wind/swell combinations and which stage of the tide might work best where. I came to realise bodyboarding was my drive, my passion. It was an integral part of who I'd become and where I'd end up. It's the same feeling shared by millions around the world, the extended family, who all crave that indescribable buzz of scooping into a round one and getting spat out.

Which brings me to the book you're holding in your hands. Whilst there had been sterling efforts pieced together online over the years and the odd magazine column punted out, there still hadn't been a comprehensive volume, ink-printed and bound, telling the story of this thing we love. So after *The Bodyboard Travel Guide* was released last year, I turned my hand to this one: the first book written on the history of bodyboarding.

That's not to say it is entirely exhaustive. It was only during the research stage that I began to appreciate the sheer scale of bodyboarding's past and the hundreds of detailed histories it has in different places around the world. To have fully included everything would have taken far longer than my deadline and word count permitted, so I had to pick the characters, stories, moments and locations that I felt best encapsulated the history of bodyboarding - from 1971 to where we are today.

Yes, there are untold stories, unmentioned figures and unreported moments, indeed things you may feel are almost criminal to have left out – and you're probably right – but this is where the line has been drawn, for this edition at least. I wanted to give green newbies an accessible overview of the sport they will grow to love, frothing groms a detailed understanding of their roots, and seasoned veterans an enjoyable boogie down memory lane... hopefully I've achieved some of this.

Read and be enriched.

– **Owen Pye**

# foreword

**Bodyboarding is perhaps the oldest form of surf craft riding, however it wasn't until the early 1970's that the inventor genius Tom Morey shaped a piece of packaging foam in a way that changed everything for the millions of wave riders that followed.**

The modern bodyboard was born; a soft flexible craft that opened the door to entirely new ways to ride waves and in so doing, new realities in waves previously deemed unrideable. What spawned from this amazingly elegant invention was beyond a good idea, a product or even a sport – it was a lifestyle. For many it became a life's quest, the bodyboard became a vehicle for a life journey in pursuit of a better understanding of personal limits and the natural world we live in.

Bodyboarders continued to evolve within the sport itself. Today's top riders are not only some of the planet's most gifted athletes, but perhaps some of the greatest wave riders that have ever lived. Beyond these accolades, however, lies a simple motivation that seems to have more purity in its mission – not for the money but rather for the experience and lifestyle that it brings. This humble purpose has built great character and remained constant since the first bodyboarders took up this discipline, but maybe most importantly it has created some great humans in the process.

For the first time, we now have a book of the sport's history... Owen Pye has written an epic chronicle.

*– Mike Stewart*

# Tom Morey

## *The Founder*

The sport of bodyboarding owes its growth and success to one man, Tom Morey. His creativity, determination and vision laid the foundation for a humble movement which in four decades has exploded into an extreme sport enjoyed by millions worldwide. This is his story, and how bodyboarding as we know it was born.

**Whilst very few sports can trace their ancestry back to one person, bodyboarding has a Mr Thomas Hugh Morey to thank for tinkering with a block of foam in 1971, and effectively modernising what ancient Polynesians had done for thousands of years.** That desire to advance developed into a thriving global sport, a stand-alone industry and indeed an entire lifestyle, changing untold people's lives. Think about that for a minute. If bodyboarding didn't exist, how many good friends would you not have? How many amazing places in the world might you not have visited? There are tens of thousands of people who have built their lives around bodyboarding, or launched a career because of it... from professional riders, shapers, judges and writers to photographers, videographers, contest organisers and entrepreneurs. Even surfing owes much to its little brother: Kelly Slater was a bodyboarder as a youngster, would he have grown to be the surfer he is without it?

Born in 1935 and a descendent of the Dodge brothers (founders of the car company that brought you the Coronet, the Charger, and the Challenger) Tom and his family upped sticks and moved from Detroit, Michigan, to Laguna, California, when he was 8 years old. Taking immediately to the ocean, he learned to bodysurf on his father's back and it wasn't long before he was hooked. Growing up on the sunny coastline in post-war California, Tom became a promising young musician and surfer, and even graced the cover of *Surfer magazine* in 1964.

During his twenties Tom worked in various aspects of composite manufacturing and engineering at Douglas Aircraft, as a salesman in the resistant materials industry around Los Angeles, and served time with the California National Guard. His love of surfing and shaping was never far away however, and in 1964 he quit the corporate world to experiment with surfboard design and manufacture in Ventura.

One day in 1969 Tom was surfing at Doheny Beach Park when he was impressed by a young surfer riding a homemade four-foot-long board made from several four-inch wide polyethylene logs. "There was nothing like it at the time," Tom said. "This kid had something unique. I went up to him and said 'That's a neat idea, but your shape's all wrong'." By this time Tom had built a reputation as an innovative shaper in California, but in 1971 – still not satisfied with life – he moved to Hawaii to pursue his dream of becoming a professional jazz drummer.

Alongside his music, the move allowed his shaping creativity to run wild. He began to experiment with a variety of board designs, including development of the prone board idea he'd seen a couple of years earlier. His first design was a failure: a six-foot board with skegs, an epoxy glass bottom and soft polyethylene deck whose nose broke off as he was paddling it out at Honolulu. A couple of months later, after he had moved to a house on the Big Island, Tom decided to make something out of his last nine-foot piece of foam. Working out of his garage – and after agonising for weeks about whether to cut it into two or three pieces – he opted for the former and cut the block in half. "There was no turning back at that point," said Tom. "Plus I found that I could shape the foam using an iron if I put a sheet of the Honolulu Advertiser down on it first (to stop the foam melting and getting sticky)... later that night, I drew a few curves on the foam with a red marker pen and went to bed."

Tom got up early on 7 July, 1971, and cut and ironed out his shape: four-and-a-half feet long, wide as possible for strength, with a square nose so he could hold on to it, and with a sharp trailing edge so the water would break away rapidly. As soon as it was finished he ran across the road to a break called Honels, on the west side of the Big Island, and took it for a spin. What he experienced in the 2ft onshore mess that day is what you sense every time you go bodyboarding. "I could actually feel the wave through the board," he said. "On a surfboard you're not feeling every nuance of the wave, but with my creation I could feel everything. I was thinking 'It turns, it's durable, it can be made cheaply, it's lightweight, it's safe...God, this could be a really big thing!'"

For Tom, developing the bodyboard was relatively easy. The hard task now was to make it into a commercial proposition and market it to the public. By this time he had joined the Baha'i faith, a religion that stresses the spiritual unity of all mankind, and which required him to give up alcohol, drugs, extra-marital sex and other worldly pleasures. It was his Baha'i friends who would lend him some seed capital to enable him to put the next stage of development into action. In late 1971 he headed back to California with $1,000 in his pocket to hawk his invention around the surf industry. After going down several dead ends, Larry Smith of G&S Surfboards offered Tom a deal, and he set about marketing his creation in earnest.

One of the first things Tom needed was a name. His first idea was to call it the S.N.A.K.E., which stood for 'Side, Navel,

The First boogie
"1971"

Arm, Knee, Elbow', or all the parts of the body you used to ride it. But after several female employees at G&S turned their noses up at it, 'Eww, yuck, I don't like snakes!' Tom came up with 'Boogie', a type of music that was popular before the Second World War. As Tom put it: "Boogie swung, and it had a wiggle and a jiggle to it... it was perfect." Returning again to California in 1973, his breakthrough came when he visited the Wilshire foam factory and saw some skins lying around ready to be thrown out. "The company would skin a block of foam," said Tom, "and these scrap pieces were like the crusts of a loaf of bread." He was allowed to take a couple of pieces away, and found that he could glue them to his board to make a slicker bottom. The Boogie Board was finally ready for action. Tom decided to go it alone and persuaded *Surfer magazine* to let him place an advertisement on credit as he had very little cash and had no way to pay for it up front. He set the price of his first board at $37 (matching his age), hoping it would cover his costs and turn a profit.

What happened next was extraordinary. On the very first day after the magazine had come out Tom checked his mailbox and found one order. The next day there were five. Finally he was in business, he trademarked the name for $10, and the Morey Boogie Board was born. Tom continued advertising with Surfer and after a few months was churning out dozens of boards a week, but he hated the fumes he was breathing from

scale up production from his wife's kitchen table, and took on friend Germaine 'Jim' Faivre. Jim had been an old sea captain, was an expert carpenter, and had a highly problem-solving, practical attitude. "What I could dream up, he could build,"

*The Boogie Board was finally ready for action. Tom decided to go it alone and persuaded Surfer magazine to let him place an advertisement on credit as he had very little cash and had no way to pay for it up front. He set the price of his first board at $37 (matching his age), hoping it would cover his costs and turn a profit.*

the glue, so he put the price of the completed board up to $45 and sold it as a kit as well. This included the core, skins, tape and instructions for you to do it yourself. Still the orders flooded in.

By 1975 Tom needed to find a business partner so he could

Tom said. "Together we created the first tooling to heat-weld the deck to the core, and started to cut them with knives instead of sawing them."

Surfing a local spot by himself one day, Tom was joined

by a blond-haired kid who paddled out on one of the smaller boogie boards that he had started to produce. "He was just catching everything!" Tom remembered. "He was persistent, just catching so many waves, and so we chatted." Needing a clean-up boy at his shop, and realising he was keen and good-spirited, Tom offered him the job. He would later grow up to become the greatest bodyboarder of all time, claiming nine world titles. "I never saw him ride a full-size boogie board during the early years," Tom said. "But sure enough as years pass he starts winning everything... pretty soon he became 'heir apparent' in terms of innovating and building stuff, he was conscientious, had talent, and wanted to learn about materials and experimentation." Tom had opened the door for a life of boogie for none other than Mike Stewart, and the rest, of course, is history. "He is like my godson or something, a really great guy," Tom said. "He was my son."

By 1977 the company was making 80,000 boards per year – peaking at 1,000 per day – selling mainly within the United States. Now based in Carlsbad, California, it occupied a new factory employing 60 workers, with a further 40 in Mexico. "It was getting to be too much," Tom said. "I'm an innovator and inventor, I'm only interested to a point, after that I want to go on to the next thing." By the end of that year things took a turn for the worse as the company suffered a cash flow crisis: it had a ton of orders but not enough money to fulfill them.

When the opportunity to get rid of the business came along, Tom and his partner Jim jumped at the chance. Selling up to Kransco, a toy company, they received a healthy sum with royalties for releasing the rights to the continental United States and Canada, and later the world. Tom was retained as a consultant and helped grow the brand during the following years. Kransco owned Morey Boogie for 16 years until it was bought out by Mattel, Inc. in 1994, and later by Wham-O, Inc. "I was always amazed at how slow it took everyone to figure out how good it was," Tom said. "It was only after lots of promotion and demonstration it started to take off, but when it did, it went out of control." In the 1980s, bodyboarding became the fastest growing watersport in the world.

Despite swift growth, the development of international competitions and later the formation of the world tour, Tom feels 'boogying' is more of an art form, not a sport, and shouldn't be judged as such. "I mean you have Ben Severson, JP Patterson and Mike Stewart in the water, who is going to judge them?" He asked. "Someone not as good." Tom would rather see a spectacular exhibition of free-flowing bodyboarding than a subjectively-judged competition: "I abhor contests and who is the 'winner'... from the standpoint of commercialisation of course you have to advertise and promote, but it is so sick. I mean a guy has to hold his board up with all his stickers and names on it, vying for position? It's just puke, in my opinion there shouldn't be any sponsorship of athletes."

In 1999 Tom stopped consulting and changed his name to 'Y'. "I've been More Y all my life," he said. "I'm finally going seriously after getting rid of More, so just plain Y does it." While some saw the name change as an odd move, it merely stood to demonstrate his creativity and willingness to challenge conventions. He is one of surfing's true legends, and the founding father of these little blocks of foam we enjoy sliding around on so much. An eccentric genius but a modest man, he was once asked how he did so much in his life: "When a guy removes smoking, drinking, gambling and chasing women from his life... there's a whole lot of time to do other neat stuff."

Left: Tom's garage in 1991. He was still experimenting with new designs and shapes. Below: Tom used to sign the early Morey Boogies with glue.

# The Pioneers

Whilst bodyboarding enjoyed exponential growth throughout the 1970s, it was still largely considered a fun pastime, pioneered by isolated individuals around the world. As the decade wore on, the first crews started to emerge in California and Hawaii, and the desire for competitions increased. As the cogs of industry began to turn, a new wave of young riders emerged and took bodyboarding to a whole new level, introducing the sport to the world.

## JOE AND JACK

One of bodyboarding's original pioneers, **Joe 'Dr 360' Wolfson** was a waterman, a hero and an inspirational human being. Born on 11 July, 1949, in Brooklyn, New York, Joe relocated with

his family to Long Beach, California, in 1956. He graduated from Dominguez High School, Compton, in 1967, and went on to study for a history degree at the University of California, Los Angeles, moving to a one-bedroom apartment in the sleepy coastal town of Manhattan Beach. An avid swimmer and bodysurfer, Joe spent endless time in the ocean and was one of the first pioneers of Tom Morey's kit boards. Quickly inventing the threesixty spin – both prone and sitting up – he soon developed a reputation as a master of the sponge board in a time when stand-up surfing aggressively dominated Californian lineups.

Intelligent, easygoing and good-humoured, Joe claimed he earned his 'Dr 360' nickname because he used to bring medical supplies on remote early bodyboarding trips abroad, but his seemingly effortless ability to spin four or five times across the face of big waves no doubt helped. His adventurous spirit would see him fly out to Oahu at the first sniff of a decent windswell, and he would surf Makapu'u from dawn til dusk. He tackled Waimea Bay as early as 1974, and was also one of the first foreign bodyboarders to visit Mexico, where he was spotted nailing reverse spins at 15ft Puerto Escondido. He came to love the Mexican Pipeline so much he freed up two months a year for the place, and even co-leased a property nearby where he invited bodyboarders to stay, naturally dubbed Casa 360.

Joe was a staunch advocate of the sport from the earliest of days, and strongly supported its initial growth and continued proliferation. Before long the Doc had developed a widespread and deep-seated respect, not just for his talent on the boogie (and non-stop 12-hour sessions) but also for his life on the dry side of the shoreline. A devoted community man, from 1968 Joe worked as a professional in the field of city government for the City of Carson, Los Angeles. Spending his time mentoring young people in the South Bay area and tirelessly dedicating himself to improving his treasured Manhattan Beach, Joe became a local hero for lifesaving, pioneering public projects, and – among a myriad of other responsibilities – chairing the Cultural Arts Commission.

A polymath and philanthropist, Joe became a role model for thousands of aspiring groms throughout the 1970s and 1980s. "There just weren't enough hours in the day for him, his life was like a soap opera," close friend Bill Jacobson said of Joe's generosity and popularity. "He looked like Jesus, he acted like Jesus… and he was always walking with two beautiful women on his arm." Instantly recognisable with his big beard, bright smile and Dr 360 license plates, Joe would be in the lineup at 6am every morning regardless of his schedule. For all his accomplishments it was Joe's simple yet unparalleled love of the ocean that people remember him for the most. Ex-colleague Richard Schraier once affably described him as 'The unofficial beach bum of the world' – in truth he was also quietly a world champion bodysurfer and multiple senior bodyboard world champion.

**Jack 'Da Rippa' Lindholm** was born on Oahu to a jazz drummer father and a hula dancer mother, growing up at Palolo Valley near Waikiki. Jack was already an experienced paipo kneeboarder when he was first lent a bodyboard by

waterman friend Riley Smith at Sandy Beach in 1974. Surfing Sandy's during the mid 1970s was an open forum with no prejudice; a place where all craft were rode and welcomed in a party atmosphere. "Riley had the first one I'd ever seen," Jack said of the funny little sponge board. "So I tried it once, and instantly I was a bodyboarder." Inspired by established stand-up rider Primo Richards, Jack experimented in getting to his feet on it initially. "I was trying to get up from my knee-riding stance," he said. "I spontaneously ended up in the dropknee position and it felt good, it was fun, and it got a reaction… I was the only guy riding a bodyboard like that. I'd found my niche."

By the following year 15-year-old Jack couldn't resist Pipeline's hype any longer, and after watching Five Summer Stories with Gerry Lopez he travelled to the North Shore with friend Kalani Tassil. Greeted with 3-5ft conditions, the pair paddled out sharing one paipo board and one bodyboard. Not intimidated by its reputation, on his first Pipe wave on the bodyboard Jack sprung up to the knee and scooped into a smooth bottom turn he'd practised at Sandy Beach, leaving just enough time to catch a glimpse of a slack-jawed surfer over the shoulder. "He was freaking out looking down at me," Jack said. "He'd never seen anything like it before, he looked dumbfounded and in shock… he couldn't believe it." Although he hadn't heard it from the water, there was a big roar from the crowd on the beach that day, almost an introductory precursor to his imminent exposure – in the following years Jack effectively made the incipient sport authoritative.

In addition to being used by Tom Morey for his Morey Boogie advertisements – first in half-page black and white, later full-page colour – Jack starred in the first published editorial photo of a bodyboarder on page 99 of the 1977 April/

Above: **Kavan Okumura** was one of the original Sandy Beach crew and is credited with inventing the invert. Mike Stewart and many others cite him as an early influence, but his career was cut short after a shoulder injury sustained in a wipeout.
Right: **Pat Caldwell**, inventor of the el rollo.

Left: **Joe Wolfson** at Casa 360 in Mexico.
Below: **Dr 360** drops into big Puerto Escondido. He was one of the first foreign body boarders to sample the Mexican pipeline.
Right: **JP Patterson and Mike Stewart** at Off the Wall in 1984.

May issue of *Surfer* magazine. "John Jones pulled into the Sandy Beach parking lot one day in his red Corvette," Jack said. "There was no one else out but he just set up his camera, took a few shots and left... lo and behold it made it to the magazine." The impact of the photograph was revolutionary and had true global reach – Jack even later met someone from Ecuador who had studied the shot and taught himself how to ride like him. Ultimately, John Jones' little monochrome snap of Jack squeezing himself into a glassy 2ft cover-up became an international introduction into taking the sport seriously.

In 1979 Jack was riding in bodyboarder friend Chris Lavoie's new Ford Mustang when it collided head-on with a tow truck. In the passenger seat and not wearing a seatbelt, Jack smashed the windshield with his head and technically died on the scene, but was revived by Chris who frantically pounded him on the chest. "I remember being mad at him when I came to, because he was punching me... I swore at

him and told him to stop, then slipped unconscious again and woke in the hospital," he said. Unbeknownst at the time, Jack had suffered severe internal injuries to the aorta in his heart, which remained dormant but in recent years resulted in an aneurysm, causing him to temporarily lose his voice – only the second person on record to be alerted to the symptom in this manner.

Tackling big Pipeline throughout the late 1970s, Jack was an oddity and the only sponger ruling its famous barrel on the knee. Having become universally known as 'dropknee' riding, several years passed before a Hawaiian grass-roots movement came to feel he deserved more credit for creating the style, and coined it as the 'Jack Stance'. "Because there wasn't a mob of bodyboarders behind me, the surfers didn't feel threatened by it in the early days," Jack said. "We were raising the bar and pushing each other, but it was mostly for fun in the beginning... they were the golden years for sure, back then you could score Pipe by yourself."

## PAT, BEN AND DANIEL

Born in California on 4 May, 1962, **Pat Caldwell** enjoyed a nomadic childhood, moving with his family to the Philippines when he was 4 years old to enable his father to train South Vietnamese police troops in Saigon. After a few years, Pat's father began receiving death threats in Manila, and in 1969 he evacuated the family to Hawaii, where Pat grew up. At 12 years old Pat was given a Morey kit board – the first year they came out – and by the following year had entered the Boogie Board division of the Sandy Beach Bodysurfing Championships. A natural in the water, Pat had become quite accustomed to the ways of the Boogie and soon began experimenting with rotating the board off the top of the lip – struggling not to land on his head.

In 1978 at the age of 16, Pat won the competition at Sandy Beach and several months later went on to land the first roll there in front of dropknee pioneer Jack. "I wanted to call it the three-dimensional threesixty," Pat said, after seeing an

Left: Jack 'da Rippa' Lindholm taming second reef pipeline in the mid 1990s.
Top right: Pat Caldwell riding the 'wounded duck' pose at Sandy Beach, Oahu.
Bottom right: Pat at the Scott Hawaii contest at Manhattan Beach in the summer of 1983. Mike Stewart helped shape the board on Pat's driveway. They shaved down the top rail to see if it slipped through the water more easily when turning. Scott Hawaii was Morey's major rival in the early 1980s.
Bottom left: Jack in 1985.

article on future moves in a 1974 issue of Surfer. "But Jack sort of laughed and said: 'Hey Pat what do you call that thing, the 'el rollo'?' So I said sure, that's a good name for it."

For Pat, growing up as a white boy in Hawaii meant he was humble from a very young age. "As the minority you didn't want to stand out or make a big deal out of stuff because negative things could happen to you," he said. "But inventing the roll in Hawaiian waters in front of Hawaiian kids was groundbreaking, I really felt at that time I was becoming accepted... we were right there at the beginning of the whole movement, and to me, creating a move like that meant I was close to being able to call myself an equal to the likes of Jack."

**Ben Severson** was born in California on 29 August, 1964, and moved to Oahu when he was six months old. Learning to surf at Waikiki by the age of 8, he was exposed to a variety of different wave-riding vehicles but within three years had gravitated towards Morey's new Boogie Boards. By 1978 Ben had begun taking trips out to the growing bodyboarding Mecca of Sandy Beach, by now a favourite break for the blossoming sport. "It was just the right place at the right time," Ben said. "There weren't a lot of us out there, and it was lucky as it allowed us to progress manoeuvres unimpeded... we didn't have to battle it out on the North Shore, we had our own little spot to do whatever we wanted."

**Daniel Kaimi** was born on Oahu on 20 May, 1962, and grew up at Kaneohe on the east side. He began bodyboarding at 15 years old after selling an old diving wetsuit to raise enough money to buy the pre-built Morey 132 BE. Learning to ride at Sandy Beach, Daniel flourished in the punishing shorebreak with Pat Caldwell, Ben Severson and Keith Sasaki, and by 1978 already felt set to test himself on the North Shore. Hitchhiking the 35 miles to Pipeline by himself, Daniel soon joined the already established Jack as two of the only regular bodyboarding faces in the lineup, especially when it got big.

"I'd heard a lot about the place and it was certainly bigger than Sandy's, but it wasn't as steep, or as shallow as Half Point," Daniel said. "Sandy's was the ultimate training ground for Pipe, it made it seem easier... all I had to do was adapt to the size." And adapt he did – on a stretch of coastline dominated largely by surfers during the late 1970s and early 1980s, Daniel made a name for himself by tackling the biggest waves on the biggest days, earning him huge respect and virtually guaranteeing him more waves when the swell dropped and the crowds came back.

## TEAM MOREY

Pat Caldwell landed his first el rollo at Pipeline in December 1980, at the Surecraft Coca-Cola Bodyboarding Championships, the first ever professional bodyboarding event at Pipe. Despite pulling the futuristic roll in the final – and getting photos published of it in *Action Now* magazine – he lost to big-wave specialist JP Patterson, who picked up the $1,000 prize and a trip for two to the North Shore. The following year Morey Boogie's marketing director Patti Serrano wanted to put together a Hawaiian team of pro riders and contacted Hawaii sales rep Roger Cundall, who helped her pick Pat Caldwell, Ben Severson, Daniel Kaimi and Keith Sasaki as the fresh faces of the company.

It was spring 1981, and on $50-per-month deals with up to eight free boards a year, the team began promotional work with the California-based photographer Craig Libuse. As well as the company's staff photographer, Craig Libuse was also the graphic artist who designed many of the early logos and adverts for Morey Boogie. Gaining recognition, that summer the team began travelling to California to partake in the Morey Boogie Jamboree series and compete in the annual Pro/Am, held at Oceanside. Morey's jamboree events were part of a powerful marketing push to get people into the sport in the early 1980s, where a tent and banner were erected at a

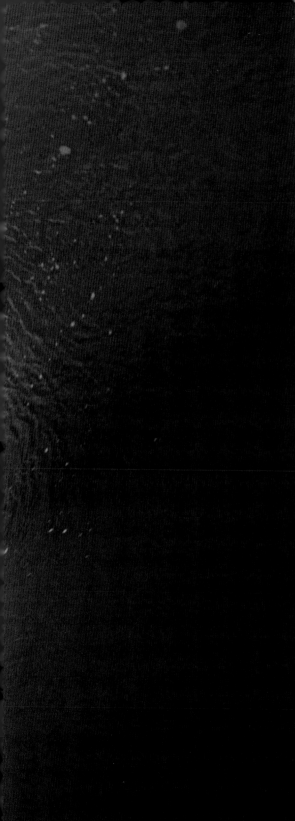

Left: Ben Severson at an outer-island shorey in the early 1980s.
Right: **March 1985, on the set of the shoot for** Morey's national TV advertisement.

beach to spread the word and give the public a chance to learn to bodyboard with the pro team.

In April 1982, the Morey crew were surfing Sandy Beach one day when a blond-haired kid named Mike Stewart arrived. For some reason he was sporting the new Mach 7-7, a board so new that, to the team's knowledge, only they had seen it – little did they know Mike had a direct connection with Tom Morey on the Big Island. "We'd never met the guy," Ben said. "Us three had just got the first samples, but here he is at Sandy's with another Mach 7. We said 'Hey who's this haole guy down the beach with a board? How'd this kid get one?' Then he paddled out and just destroyed the place, we were like 'Whoa, who are you?!?'... that was our introduction to Mike Stewart."

Mike rode the board in his first competition and had it dialled. "I was like Tom's personal test pilot over there," he said. "He sent me that board when I was on the mainland to try, I brought it back and competed on it for the first time... it was the first prototype Mach 7 with super big rails and a flat tail." The team didn't know it at the time, but the revolutionary slick-bottomed boards they were now riding had been tested and developed by Mike for a number of years on the Big Island. By the next summer he was on the team, and living with Keith Sasaki in San Clemente, California.

**JAY REALE AND THE 1982 WORLD CHAMPIONSHIPS**
Jay Reale was born 12 February, 1964, and grew up in isolated Maryland – 1,000 miles north of the bodyboarding hub of the East Coast in Florida. Learning to ride waves on inflatable air mattresses, Jay got his first taste of an actual bodyboard in the summer of 1979, receiving a Morey Pro-Line Red Edge that Christmas, and competing on it locally the following year. Having noticed the popularity of the boards increase, in 1981 Jay wrote letters to the Eastern Surfing Association (ESA) asking it to create a bodyboarding division for its amateur championships. The lobbying worked, and the following year bodyboarders up and down the East Coast flocked to the event in August – the first proper bodyboarding event many had ever experienced. Jay won the division, beating none

other than future 11-times world surfing champion Kelly Slater in the process, and earned himself an invitation to the inaugural Sunkist International Morey Boogie Bodyboard Pro Championships to be held in Hawaii that December.

The competition was an incredible success. Top riders from around the world were picked by international distributors and put up collectively in condos on the North Shore by Morey, which had correctly hoped mixing the international riders together would spark a healthy vibe during the event. With great foresight, it also captured the entire waiting period and competition on videocamera, forever preserving on tape the thrills, spills and golden moments of the unprecedented contest. For many it was the first time they had ever met, mingled with their heroes on the pro team, or ever seen the North Shore deliver its famous lines of thunder.

The first day after arriving Pipeline was breaking at Second Reef, and the group was brought down to the beach to watch it break while Mike Stewart, JP Patterson, Daniel Kaimi and Jack Lindholm paddled out. "The international riders were petrified," Jay said. "We couldn't even fathom what Daniel Kaimi was doing out there, taking off on huge bombs and spinning down these huge faces... it was such an eye-opener, those guys rode it like a 2ft beachbreak." For many of the international riders who hadn't visited Hawaii before, coming to terms with waves like these required a short, steep learning curve and a healthy dose of courage. "Oh it was fun," Daniel said. "I had no idea about what the others guys from around the world rode, I was just thinking 'Well, this is my backyard, so let's go out there and play.'"

Entering a four-day window between Christmas and New Year, the first day of trials was held at a large, stormy Pipeline, and the second day was switched to Makaha on the west side. In the small shorey, Mike Stewart, Jay Reale and other amped boogers messed around in the sunshine, running and skimming their boards, trying snappy cutbacks into the dumping, sandy wash. Out back, those still competing – including Lisa Miller, the only woman in the event – rode long, mushy rights, banking spins and attempting sloppy rolls. On the third and final day however, the event returned to a sunny Pipeline, cleanly breaking at 6-8ft Hawaiian – which, as many riders were finding out, meant 15ft faces.

Despite the absence of Ben Severson, who was sporting four pins in his ring finger after crushing it between a car door and a wall the month before, and Pat Caldwell, who had his final University of Hawaii exams that day, 24 riders took to the four quarterfinals in six-man heats. As expected, the locals dominated in the conditions, with Mike Stewart busting his trademark projected rolls and Jack Lindholm ripping through deep dropknee tubes. "They were just playing with the waves," Jay said. "None of us had ever seen someone get launched out with the lip with an el rollo before, at that point everybody would just go to the top of the wave, flop over and go back down... we were just sitting on the beach blown away." Despite largely dominating the heats, even the Hawaiians paid their dues on occasion. Prior to the semis, afro-haired Daniel Kaimi took off too deep on one wave and took a beating, scraping his hip, getting his shorts ripped down to his ankles and ending up down near Ehukai. After a long paddle back he changed his game plan to wait for the big ones, making a couple and finishing the heat third, progressing through.

With the majority of the crowd on the beach consisting of the riders and their respective friends and family, the vibe was electric. From the small scaffolding of the judging tower, event director Bob Thomas announced the action alongside his fellow judges, which included a frustrated Ben Severson still nursing his mangled finger. The buzz was amped as almost every wave was watched and cheered from takeoff to pull off, and even Hawaiian pro surfer and event water patrolman Marvin Foster – who was meant to be keeping surfers out of the lineup – was taking off on free waves to get a piece of the action.

Jay paddled out in his heat terrified, and after 15 minutes of the 25 he still hadn't caught a wave. Alone on the outside he finally had a perfect peak swing his way, but despite some Marvin Foster words of encouragement 'Go brah! Go!! What are you doing?!?!' He scratched over the top, too scared to make the drop. "I remember thinking 'Man I've spent all this money coming over here, I'll be so bummed if I don't at least try to take off on something'," Jay said. "So I finally took a wave, bottom turned, pulled up into a little tube and came out buzzing with adrenaline, I couldn't wait for the next one. Unfortunately my confidence got the better of me, and the next one just smashed me flat on my back underwater, dragged me over the reef with my rashie over my head, and ripped one of my fins off, it put me right back in my place."

Jay finished fifth in his heat and didn't progress – something he was thankful for at the time. Veteran Jack Lindholm won the heat with his precision 'Jack Stance' barrels and progressed through the semi into the final, where he beat

Above: The 1986 Morey World Championships: (L to R) Jack Lindholm, Mike Stewart, Keith Sasaki, JP Patterson, Pat Caldwell and winner Ben Severson. In the background is Bob Thomas, long time technical director for the event. Up until the mid 1990s competitors were obliged to ride a Morey board in the event, usually a Mach 7. In this shot JP Patterson is holding a Mach 10.
Left: Pat Caldwell charging Waimea Shorebreak in the mid 1990s.

Mike Stewart into second, finishing behind Daniel Kaimi. The big-wave hellman got barrelled on virtually every wave he caught and began landing his rolls out of the tube for more points. "After I got through the semis my friend Philip Helfrich told me the judges couldn't see me landing my rolls in the barrel," Daniel said. "He told me I had to make my rolls a little more visible as they couldn't give me points for something they couldn't see... it was the best coaching I ever got, he helped me win the contest." Interestingly Daniel had actually failed to get through the trials at Makaha, but after a recalculation of the scores he was awarded a second chance to compete at Pipe for the final day. He duly obliged of course, and took the crown as the first official world champion. "Before the event I hadn't really cared for the contest scene, but it was

*The buzz was amped as almost every wave was watched and cheered from takeoff to pull off, and even Hawaiian pro surfer and event water patrolman Marvin Foster – who was meant to be keeping surfers out of the lineup – was taking off on free waves to get a piece of the action.*

awesome and exciting when they announced the names out," Daniel said. "I'd only ever been in a few competitions up to that point, but winning that event was like a dream come true."

Jay's invitation to the competition opened up his entire perspective on the sport, and started a long and illustrious career for the East Coaster. After his heat he realised that to have a chance of competing with the Hawaiians at all he would have to return to the North Shore each year. "That event changed my entire life path," Jay said. "It was a groundbreaking event, not just for me... it started bodyboarding as a high-performance sport at an international level." From that point on, riders from around the globe would converge each season on the North Shore to catch up, compare notes and see how they stacked up against each other after another year of disparate progression.

Meanwhile on the US mainland there were growing hotbeds of bodyboarders in California and the East Coast, and with Morey's promotions coordinator Patti Serrano hot on the case for new talent, bodyboarding had begun to flourish. By the early 1980s events such as the Morey jamborees and national contests had exposed the sport to many more people. "Where Hawaii was becoming the crème de la crème of the world scene, competing at a Morey Nationals event was already the equivalent in the US," Jay said. As soon as he won the inaugural ESA contest, Jay began lobbying to add East Coasters to the national event. Morey obliged, and after he competed at his first Morey Nationals event in the summer of 1983, East

quarters of the way in, leaving flex in the nose but stiffening the tail. He then sealed the rod in with a hot glue gun from Sears – fixing his problem, but perhaps more importantly creating a working stringer prototype for the industry too. Within a couple of years JP had progressed to experimenting shaping the bottom, creating channels in 1986, and by then also strengthening Scott Hawaii's cores with defective club shafts supplied by golf companies.

Three years after the Morey Mach 7-7 brought with it a revolutionary shift in equipment, *Bodyboarding* magazine was introduced by former world champion surfer Peter Townend and Newport Wedge kneeboarder Bill Sharp. It was a big moment. Finally the sport had its own dedicated publication, which not only provided an outlet for photographers and enabled a forum for bodyboard news, but

## EXPLORATION, BOARD DESIGN, MEDIA AND THE BOOM

In 1983, shortly after the Pipe contest had ended, Daniel Kaimi became one of the first bodyboarders to make the trek to the mystical G-Land in Java, Indonesia. However, it wasn't all plain sailing for the inaugural world champion. The boat captain he and his mates picked for the mission actually had no idea how to dodge sets through the channel into the bay. "We chose this one guy who looked like Charles Bronson to take us, as we figured he would be tough and know what to do," Daniel said. "But once we were out there he started freaking out and crying, and as soon as a set came he turned the boat sideways to it... we started shouting 'No! Go, go, go!' and were fighting with the guy to get it pointing in the right direction, man it was so close, we just made it over the top!" In the end the risk was worth the reward – Daniel lucked into some of the best conditions G-Land had ever produced, with the swell peaking at 15ft. "The waves were so good my cheeks hurt from smiling so much," Daniel said. "Despite getting bigger, it was best at a solid 8-10ft. All the sections were linking up all the

Coasters were soon given a chance to qualify in competitions organised on their own side of the country.

After the release of the first slick-bottomed board, the Morey Mach 7-7, (which only the American riders in the opening world championships had as it had not been distributed overseas yet), bodyboarders enjoyed a huge increase in speed, manoeuvrability and projection. By 1984 Ben Severson had started experimenting with transitional rails and altering the size of his boards as well. In bigger surf he had found the shapes too crude for his 5'6" frame, and began shortening his templates so he had a version he could ride more comfortably at Pipeline. With help from JP Patterson – who shaped his first one – Ben received laminated blanks boxed from Morey Boogie to play around with himself in shaping the rails and tails, adhering the skins and testing them on the North Shore.

By this time Daniel Kaimi had also begun to experiment in increasing the strength of the Moreys, having snapped several of his boards in quick succession. Heating up a round aluminium rod, he pounded it into the board about three-

From 1977 until 1981 Morey Boogie's promotional manager Patti Serrano organised contests and jamborees in California, on the east coast of the USA and in Hawaii. These events were instrumental in making bodyboarding ever more popular. PHOTOS COURTESY PATTI SERRANO.

Above: Jack Lindholm, Ben Severson and Mike Stewart cram in the back of a hire car on a trip to Molokai in April 1983.

Right: Jack shacked at Uluwatu, in 1987.

Above right: Chris Ann Kim, Ben Severson, Dean Marzol, Danny Kim and Mike Stewart.

Below: This kind of attire was considered fashionable in 1983! JP Patterson and Pat Caldwell. Check the bodyboard handles plugged into their boards!

In the early days bodyboarders relied on the mainstream surf media, which mostly consisted of US magazines *Surfer* and *Surfing* for photos of top riders. These magazines were distributed worldwide and did much to spread the word. In 1985 *Surfing* carried out some reader research and discovered that a quarter of their readers were into bodyboarding. They therefore decided to launch *Bodyboarding* magazine as a special issue. It was a great success, became a quarterly magazine the following year and bi-monthly in 1987, contributing greatly to the bodyboarding boom of the era. However, the downturn of the early 1990s saw it reduced to a single issue. It was relaunched towards the end of the decade but was a shadow of its former self and faded away a few years later.

Left: **Keith Sasaki**, west side of Oahu in the late 1980s.
Right: **Hauoli's frog-legged roll at Off the Wall.**
Hauoli Reeves was one of the great characters during bodyboarding's boom times back in the late 1980s and early 1990s, famous for his aerial style and partying.
Far right: **Fooling around on the west side of Oahu with (L-R) Seamas Mercado, Hauoli Reeves, Ben Severson and Chris Ann Kim.**

showed a living could be made from the sport if you had the skills to match your ambitions. At this time videographer Tom Boyle had also begun making bodyboarding films, which allowed groms to play, rewind and study the top riders – vastly increasing the rate of development. "Video made everything happen," Ben said. "It helped guys who lived in far off places learn to ride, it was key, it helped build bodyboarding." Jay agrees: "It accelerated the progression of the sport by leaps and bounds... suddenly guys in isolated beaches in the UK, Portugal or Maryland could learn in slow-mo what took us years of trial and error."

By the mid 1980s Joe Wolfson was director of the Scott Hawaii Bodyboarding Tour, and alongside the jamborees had introduced a special all-star clinic at Huntington Beach, California. Top riders such as Mike Stewart and Pat Caldwell were invited to help the sport grow at grass roots level, giving tips and advice in riding to the excited crowds. "We had two somewhat shy legends open up and speak like college

professors on a subject they had both studied for over 20 years," Joe said of the event. Conversely, Daniel Kaimi had never been a fan of the jamborees in the small Californian conditions, instead focusing on freesurfing big waves on the North Shore and pushing himself when things got heavy. "I always believed Christ protected me, so I would go," Daniel said of how his faith affected his mindset in the water. "If I made it, I was having fun, if I didn't make it, I would go to heaven."

### JP AT WAIMEA BAY: 42 INCHES VS 57 FEET

In 1985 another of Hawaii's big-wave aficionados, JP Patterson, survived a 50ft rogue wave at Waimea Bay, going down in history as one of the biggest waves a bodyboarder had ever faced. JP grew up in Hawaiian surfing culture, and recognised from an early age that whoever caught the biggest waves – and was humble in doing so – got the most respect. However, if making his bones as a big-wave bodyboarder wasn't hard enough, JP had the added problem of relearning how to

handle his board after chopping half of his right thumb off in a circular saw accident in October, 1982. In line for a $10,000 payout in workers' compensation, JP was more concerned with the 45 days he had left to get the stump healed and working for the inaugural world championships at Pipeline. "Nobody

expected me to heal up in time for that first event, especially Ben Severson," JP said. "He was a little punk back then and kept saying 'Oh JP won't be in the contest, he won't be in the contest, there's no way, it's impossible'... so he was most surprised when I showed up ready to go." In the following period JP trained intensely, pushed his comfort level and often waited out back for hours for the right one, becoming a familiar face in North Shore lineups when things got sizey. Easily spotted riding in his reverse 'wounded duck' style (outside hand on the nose, inside hand on the deck, common also to Pat Caldwell), respect for the thumbless, skinny white boy grew accordingly.

On 18 January, 1985, the then 25-year-old arrived at Waimea Bay in the morning and watched a huge swell develop and grow bigger throughout the day. Unlike many large

Waimea swells which crumble, offering the rhino-chasing stick figures a feathering drop into a long, drawn out bottom turn, the amount of west in the swell was making these jacking mountains break top-to-bottom. Coupled with a huge sandbar which had shifted outwards over the day due to the heavily-eroded beach, a powerful current had developed. This rip was so strong it took renowned big-wave surfer Ken Bradshaw three entire laps of the bay –more than an hour of swimming – to get back to shore after losing his board.

Around 3pm the lineup had become empty, and veteran Waimea surfer James 'Booby' Jones announced he was thinking of going out. JP swiftly said he'd join him, grabbed his Scott Hawaii bodyboard and custom ¼" thick leash, and the pair sat on the beach for 45 minutes timing the sets. "The shorebreak

Above: **JP Patterson in full flight at The Wedge in California. Check out the webbed gloves, these were highly popular in the late 1980s and early 1990s.**

Kainoa McGee evolved from skinny Hawaiian grom in the mid 1980s to menacing Pipeline enforcer in the 1990s, famously dealing out beatings to those who transgressed the unwritten rules of Pipeline etiquette. It was this image, as well as his fearless charging at Pipeline (he first surfed it at the age of 15), which endeared him to bodyboarders the world over. A four-time Pipe world championship runner-up, in 2001 Kainoa evolved again, and started standup surfing. In 2003 he made it to the semi finals of the Hansen's Energy Pro at Pipeline, beating Shane Beschen along the way. He is now an international star of the stand-up paddle boarding scene.

Left and above: Paul Roach exploded onto the scene in 1990 at the tender age of 17. Hailing from Encenitas in California, he rode almost exclusively dropknee, shunned contests and developed a punk-ass rebelious image. His aggressive tail-flinging style and lay-backs were highly influential, and he even featured in an early Taylor Steele standup movie, alongside Kelly Slater.

Hard to believe in these days of websites and social media, but back in the 1980s and 1990s, magazine advertising was the main method companies used to reach their customer. During the boom, *Bodyboarding* was stuffed with ads from mainstream surfing brands as well as bodyboard brands. Top row left to right: **Keith Sasaki / O'Neill 1988, Sasaki / Reef 1991, Kauai Classic Team / Challenger 1991, Seamas Mercado / Billabong 1990.** Bottom row: **Ben Severson / BZ 1990, Danny Kim / Airwalk 1988, Jack Lindholm / Quiksilver 1988.**

was unbelievable," JP said. "It wasn't even a shorebreak, it was more like a beachbreak, with 20ft+ faces." With declining intervals as the swell increased, the pair sucked it up, gunned their paddle and made it out – into the biggest surf JP had ever experienced. Trying to line up their markers in unprecedented conditions, the pair were joined 45 minutes later by Mark Foo and Alec 'Ace Cool' Cooke, and the foursome began to take on the monsters.

By now around a thousand people had stopped what they were doing and lined the beach and Kamehameha Highway to watch the widow-makers breaking from the point all the way across the bay. "It was like the Roman gladiator days," JP said. "We were like Christians being thrown to the lions." Catching a 30ft one, JP bottom turned and trimmed out to its mammoth shoulder, before aiming a big cutback to ride it into the shorebreak and get in. Not making the link to the inside section, he turned and headed back out for another. "We were all on edge, all watching the horizon, and it was getting a

little dark," he said. "All of a sudden we heard the crowd start to yell, scream and whistle, and we were wondering what was going on... there was of course a set coming. We made it over the first and second waves, but the third one was rogue, it had stacked a couple on top of each other, and it broke left, a hundred yards further out than the others... we all started scratching for it, them on their 9 and 10ft guns, me on my 42 inch bodyboard." Leashless, James Jones was first up, stood on his board and dived under just before it thunderously unloaded, leaving Alec Cooke – and further back Mark Foo and JP – to deal with a bouncing avalanche of whitewater. Unlike Jones, Foo had two 9ft leashes tied together, and not wanting to become entangled with them, JP kicked away from him to brace for the biggest duckdive of his life.

Unable to unstrap his leash in time, JP rolled off his board only to penetrate around 4ft underwater when he was hit. "It was like being a cockroach in a washing machine if someone was to hit the spin cycle," he said. "It went from

TOM BOYLE

calm to instantly dark and uncontrolled, it was trying to pull me apart, I span and tumbled so deep I could have been 50ft underwater, my ears were popping, I just kept tumbling... I started thinking at least I didn't die in a car crash, that I would get respect for having died doing something I loved, and that I wonder if it hurts when you drown, all this stuff... but then it started to dissipate and relinquish, and I suddenly realised I had to find which way the surface was."

Thirty feet underwater and completely out of air, JP began swimming upwards towards the light. "I was so scared that I'd get two inches from the surface just in time for another to land on me as I'd been down so long," he said. Fortunately he broke the surface to find a fizzing calm: "It was like that wave had sucked the whole ocean flat," he said. What no one knew at that point was that before the quartet had even started scratching to get over it, the lifeguards had already called the fire department to get the helicopter in the air to rescue them. Before it thrummed into sight JP had spotted his board and swam to retrieve it from the middle of the bay. Stuck in the impact zone and tiring quickly, JP had to battle bulldozer lines of white water and was soon sucked across to Jump Rock on the west side of the bay. With yet another set about to break, he let go of his board and ducked under several more, before a helicopter rescue basket landed right next to him and allowed him a breathless vertically escape to the beach. Ken Bradshaw later estimated the wave to have been 57ft.

## GOING PRO, THE PSAA AND A MAGICAL DISCOVERY

By 1985 bodyboarding had grown to the point that it was added to almost every surfing association district on the US coastline – from California and Hawaii to the Gulf and East Coasts. "Every amateur's dream was to become your association champion, US Amateur Champion and the Morey National Champion," Jay Reale said. While the blossoming Pipeline comp was predominantly to showcase professional bodyboarding, amateur riders were also allowed to compete, as the very concept of pro riding hadn't yet made it to some of the countries which entered. Jay rode as an amateur throughout the early and mid 1980s, but after graduating in 1986 was faced with a choice: to go into teaching, or up sticks and try to make a living from bodyboarding. The following year he moved to California, accepted $200 prize money in a competition at Ventura and became a professional rider.

In the meantime Ben Severson's board alterations had worked, and he was fast becoming recognised as a key figure in bodyboarding's growth and technical development. In 1986 he enjoyed his most successful competition year in his career, winning both the Morey World Championship and National Pro/Am titles. The following year, after coming away from a foam manufacturer trade show to negotiate the introduction of his own line of boards, Ben began talks with Bobby Szabad's brand BZ. The Californian company showed great interest in Ben's vision of customised shapes and templates, and quickly signed him up to a big employee contract which included a $1,500-per-month salary, royalties, benefits, medical insurance and full travel expenses. After joining BZ, Ben wasted little time in releasing his first custom board, the BEN T-10. The model, despite retailing at $305, became one of the best selling and most sought-after signature boards on the market. "It was the turning point for me, we'd numbered them from 0-1,000 because the owner never thought I'd sell that many," Ben said. "We went through that number in under two years and stopped numbering them after that." The move to BZ opened up his career and meant he was soon earning $80,000 per annum whilst honing and testing 20-30 boards a year.

The burgeoning bodyboarding movement was not overlooked by the Professional Surfing Association of America (PSAA), which by this point had latched on to the phenomenon and added it to its televised Bud Tour events. Despite mixed opinion of whether the weak, small-wave venues were helping its reputation, the sport was now in people's living rooms a minimum of eight times a year.

Then in 1986, Ben joined great rival Mike Stewart and Kauai Classic's Chris Tennberg on a ten-day PSAA trip to Tahiti against the Tahitian Surfing Federation. One day after exploring the island, the trio got to the now famous 'end of the road' to be greeted with a big reef pass and lots of white water, but no visible waves. Deciding to hang around anyway to stretch their legs after the long drive, they noticed the occasional draught of mist popping up beyond the reef. "From the road we couldn't see the wave very well because of all the white water in the way," Ben said. "So we went down the beach, and could just about make out this wave breaking and start to peel, but then it looked like it closed out. A second later we saw this huge spit blow out the back, and we looked at each other and said 'Well, if it spits, we should be able to surf it, right?'" – They had discovered Teahupo'o, the heaviest wave on the planet.

Taking advantage of a passing Zodiac demo tour, the next day Mike and Chris launched one of the boats for a spin around the island to look for some new spots. Towards the end of the day and on their way home, they came across the heavy reef at Teahupo'o, this time from the back. "At the time we didn't realise it was the same wave as we'd seen from the land," Mike said. "It was peeling barrels at 4-6ft and it was perfect, just perfect conditions. It was late afternoon, the light was hitting the land... it was paradise." Tearing themselves away from such a discovery was naturally difficult for Mike and Chris, but returning in the dark would prove to bite them on the ass, quite literally. Whilst cruising in at a pace across the sheet glass of the lagoon in falling light, they couldn't properly make out the channel markers and ended up ramming the reef. "We jumped in the water to try to dislodge the boat, but I guess there must have been fire coral or something down there because after we got back to the hostel and showered afterwards, it activated it," Mike said. "It was the itchiest sensation I've ever experienced, all down my crotch and legs, I just wanted to rip my skin off!" After it had cooled down and they'd recovered, Ben was all ears. "They claimed it had been 6ft and heavier than Pipeline," Ben said. "I was like 'Really?? There's another place like Pipeline? You promise?!?' We went the next day, it was like finding gold."

At this point the only known rider was a local Tahitian

"So we went down the beach, and could just about make out this wave breaking and start to peel, but then it looked like it closed out. A second later we saw this huge spit blow out the back, and we looked at each other and said 'Well, if it spits, we should be able to surf it, right?'"

MIKE SEARLE

CHRIS POWER

BRIAN BIELMANN

ABA INTERNATIONAL PRO AM

Top: By the mid 1990s the recession had severely curtailed the bodyboarding industry in the US, but it was just starting to boom in many other parts of the world. Contingents of boogers soon began congregating on the North Shore for the winter season. Some of the most hardcore came from South Africa: The likes of the Cockwell brothers gained a rep for charging hard and existing on little or no money. One of their most successful compatriots was Alistair Taylor, pictured here at Pipeline in 1998.

Left: Spot the bodyboarding hero in this shot after some serious fun at the famous standing wave on the Waimea River in 1988.

Far left: A 1990 contest at Manly Beach, Australia.

Right: JP Patterson fooling around at Newport Wedge.

who for years had paddled his canoe out across the lagoon to the edge of the reef to bodyboard it by himself. Following the success of that trip Ben returned to Teahupo'o more than twenty times over the next seven years. "I was competing in Santa Cruz a few years later when Poto (Tahitian surfer Vetea David) cornered me and said 'Where's this wave??' I laughed and said 'Ah wouldn't you like to know!'"

However, despite trying to keep tight-lipped about its location, on one of Ben's return trips he invited lensman Brian 'Hank' Stephan, and before long it seemed the entire surfing world knew of Teahupo'o and was scouring its whereabouts – Ben later admitted he wished he'd never brought along any photographers. Mike agreed, but said any exposure he had caused wasn't intentional: "After those shots got published it was pretty much the beginning of the end really... it wasn't malicious, but by then the cat was out of the bag."

### PAT'S RISE AND DR 360'S SHINE

By 1987 Daniel Kaimi had drifted away from professional bodyboarding to start a successful career as an automobile salesman for Nissan. At the same time, Pat Caldwell was advertised in the local paper – where more than '2,000 of his closest personal friends' would be in attendance. Despite it being tongue-in-cheek, such was his popularity that in the end that figure wasn't too far off the mark. Come 1 April, Los Angeles newspaper editors had to keep their wits about them too – a few years earlier he'd convinced a South Bay reporter to file a story on a fake sky-diving team he belonged to which required funding to make it to a fictitious world championship in Norway.

One of Joe's party tricks involved gatecrashing Hollywood premieres and being mistaken for Steven Spielberg. "He loved doing that, and I think Sunset Boulevard was the furthest he ever went from the ocean too," Pat said. "I once asked him if he'd ever visited the mountains, he said: 'No, never been, never wanted to'... he felt nervous if he ever went east of the 405 freeway". (A Los Angeles interstate around five miles from the coastline).

In addition to dozens of competition wins over his career, Joe also tirelessly worked as an event organiser, community leader and fine arts superintendent for LA city government, tour director for Scott Hawaii, and a contributing editor for

had contracts slashed or were dropped completely during this time, and were forced to leave the sport to make ends meet on land.

By the mid 1990s and with dwindling sponsorship budgets, the US domestic tour also dried up – a body blow for the sport which at the time was still very much an American-led movement. Facing a promotional crisis, it needed a grander vision to unify bodyboarding around the world, much the way surfing had done. In 1994 the Global Organisation of Bodyboarding (GOB) was born. Driven by Mike Stewart, Ben Severson, Bob Thomas and Derek Hulme, it began the task of coordinating the major international events of the day into the first world tour.

### AFTER THE HOOTER

In 1990 JP Patterson began working as a salesman for Viper fins, having modified the iconic design with shorter blades and drainage holes to make them more functional for bodyboarding. He went on to manage the Morey team, after Mike Stewart had encouraged him to take the reins when the company was bought out by Mattel.

> "After those shots got published it was pretty much the beginning of the end really... it wasn't malicious, but by then the cat was out of the bag."

getting ready to move back to California that October as he was finding it difficult travelling from Hawaii to the PSAA tour events, which were by this stage underway on both coasts of the mainland US.

The following year Pat switched sponsors to ride for Wave Rebel, and began earning the most money of his professional career, taking home $50,000-$60,000 per year from his contract, PSAA event money and royalties from his appearance riding for Morey in a Wrigley's Juicy Fruit TV commercial. The advertisement was played internationally from 1988, and featured Pat busting a roll at Pipeline along with waves from Ben, Lisa Miller and Dave Cunniff. Pat's realisation that bodyboarding had developed a cultural popularity came one day in the late 1980s when he was recognised by someone in a grocery store in Las Vegas – 300 miles from the nearest ocean.

Pat once described Joe 'Dr 360' Wolfson as having 'Been born 20 years too early.' Though at 37, the multiple senior world champion was still a force to be reckoned with on the contest scene, defeating riders like JP Patterson – 12 years his junior – with slick combinations of el rollos, backward coffins and his signature spins. Well known for his practical jokes, in 1989 Joe threw a surprise 40th birthday party for himself –

*Bodyboarding* magazine. In 1993, Californian company Ocean Storm released the 'Dr 360, 3rd Reef' signature model. Despite sporting the quality and features of many high-end boards, Joe insisted it be retailed at only $100 – around half the price of the competition – to make it affordable for kids, and those who wanted to progress but were on a budget.

### THE BUST

Whilst the sport was still booming in regions like Australia, the recession of the early 1990s played havoc in the bodyboard industry in the US, and major surf and bodyboard sponsors began dropping riders to look after their balance sheets. For Pat, the decline of Wave Rebel's international board sales meant he was soon making the move to New Wave Bodyboards, a subsidiary of BZ, and from June 1993 had to supplement his income by working as a lifeguard in San Clemente.

While some argued the larger economic downturn was to blame, many sensed several influential surf companies had began to see bodyboarding as a major threat to their markets, and decided a significant chop was necessary to keep the sport from overtaking surfing. Regardless of the exact reasons – most likely a combination of both – many professional bodyboarders

By 1996 Ben Severson had started making leashes and bodyboard accessories under his company Ben Severson Designs (BSD), using the GOB World Tour as an opportunity to market the products and establish a distribution network. When BZ changed hands he was faced with a cut contract and offered the new owners the license to make his boards. They declined, and consequently Ben left the company for Glendora manufacturer Ocean Storm. He continued to travel the world and compete on tour for the next two years, but by 1998 had retired to focus on building his brand and selling custom boards. He remains an important figure on Oahu, lifeguarding, judging and organising bodyboard events.

A multiple-title winner, Jay Reale reached fifth in the world in 1997 and retired his professional career the following year, with concurrent top-16 finishes on the GOB World Tour, Australian Tour, US Tour and the Californian BIA Tour. Unsure of what

to do next, a certain Tom Morey suggested that a new thing called the internet was about to take off, and that he might want to think about opening a shop 'online'. With six months of savings in the bank, Jay and wife Vicki heeded his wisdom and took a chance on opening the first – and subsequently to become the biggest – bodyboard shop on the web; ebodyboarding.com. An ESA All-Star, Jay competed for 17 years and went from being the sport's clean-cut poster boy to one of its leading ambassadors, helping to elevate bodyboarding's profile in both the competitive and public spheres.

Following stints riding for Toobs in 1994 and Custom X in 1995, Pat Caldwell retired from competitive bodyboarding after getting knocked out from the 1996 Pipeline event and subsequently yelling at the judges on the beach. "I'd got quite far in the comp and I got screwed," he said. "I was doing big rolls and more vertical manoeuvres in the pocket, whilst the other guy was just spinning onto the shoulder, yet somehow he beat me... I was really mad, I said 'That's it, I'm done competing'. I was so fed up with the judging and what was going on that I said from then on I would do my best to help change the way contests were judged."

He followed up on his promise, and from 1996 to 2000 Pat worked closely with respected surf judge Midget Smith, who also mentored future International Bodyboard Association (IBA) Head Judge Craig Hadden. In between photo-hunting North Shore winters and charging huge Waimea Shorey for international cover shots, Pat honed his judging skills in local

competitions, amateur contests and even World Qualifying Tour (WQT) surfing events. His hard work paid off – by the end of the 1990s the GOB's judging criteria had strayed more towards the mantra of 'the most critical manoeuvre on the most critical wave at the most critical position, performed functionally'. Pat's moment in the hot seat came when floating in the channel at Teahupo'o as one of the judges at the Tahiti Skins Event 2000. "That competition was a milestone in the sport," he said. "That forward spin Ryan Hardy did from deep in the tube was mindblowing... it was so critical, if he had blown it in that position he was going head-first into the reef. I gave him a perfect 10." Pat would go on to take the role of General Manager on the IBA World Tour.

**A LEGEND MOVES ON**

Despite having lived an astonishingly fit and healthy lifestyle, in early 1998 Joe Wolfson developed a chronic cough, and after several misdiagnoses and alternative therapies was found to have an untreatable tumour between his lungs and windpipe – possibly the result of spending so much time in the carcinogenic waters of the South Bay area of Los Angeles. Doctors gave him only a few months left to live. Facing terminal cancer and with no wife or children of his own, Joe did what came naturally to him – he helped others. Emptying almost $100,000 of savings from his bank account and 401k retirement plan, over the next few months he paid for a friend's laser eye surgery, two years of tuition at University of

California, Berkeley, for another friend's son, handed cash-filled envelopes to those close to him, and gave his worldly possessions – which were quite substantial – to numerous young people who were in need.

Years before, Joe had once told a newspaper reporter that he would bodyboard for as long as he lived, but that if the end was to come, "It'll just be one of those things where I go out into the ocean someday and don't come back." By the approaching winter of 1998 he felt it necessary to make good on his prediction. On 11 November he wrote a suicide note, left $5,000 for his farewell party and paddled out on his signature model at Manhattan Beach for one last surf. Afterwards, to avoid drifting into deeper water and being eaten by sharks, he found a buoy around 150 yards off the beach, tied himself to it and waited to die.

After a night of floating in the cold water he was spotted the next morning unconscious with severe hypothermia and a body temperature of just 81F (27C). Regaining consciousness in hospital, at first he was disappointed he hadn't died, but then read 33 letters he had been sent from local children and decided to try and fight the disease. After he left hospital he met the children and apologised. "It was the worst message in the world I could send them," he said. The following year he threw an extravagant 50th birthday party at Redondo Beach and made his annual trip to Puerto Escondido, but having reportedly turned down chemotherapy that year, his condition worsened. In the end it didn't matter. On 21 February, 2000, the man once described as both the 'Pied Piper' and 'Peter Pan of Bodyboarding' died, after his car veered off the Marina Freeway and hit a eucalyptus tree. Witnesses said the car didn't brake.

"His passion for the sport was unparalleled," Pat Caldwell said. "I'm certain he spent more hours in the water in his 50 years than anybody." For a man who grew up and flourished through the swinging sixties and psychedelic seventies, Dr 360 once claimed that salt water was 'The best drug there is'. Amen.

# Mike Stewart
## *The Godfather*

Mike Stewart is, simply put, the greatest bodyboarder of all time. Nine-times world champion, Mr Pipeline was the international face of the sport and dominated competitions throughout the 1980s and early 1990s. A pioneer of big-wave surfing and inventor of new manoeuvres, Mike drew the blueprints, dug the foundations and laid the blocks of modern day bodyboarding, influencing hundreds of thousands in the process. Despite knocking on the door of his sixth decade, the Hawaiian still competes on the world tour at the highest level, routinely beating other riders who grew up with posters of him on their bedroom walls.

Stewart eyes his landing from a textbook apporach to the lip.

The king at home, January, 1987.

Born on 17 May, 1963, Mike Stewart grew up on the island the world's surf fraternity gather each year to prove themselves – Oahu. The middle brother of three, Mike's love of waveriding began at 5 years old on the east side of the island, riding chunks of Styrofoam in the short-period windchop the trades whipped up on the beaches. His natural talent flourished after he received a Morey Boogie kit board at 10 years old, and soon it was the natural thing for Mike to spend whole weekends in the ocean near his home at Nuuanu. "It was a paradigm shift, I rode that thing for three years straight until '76," Mike said. "No stringer, EVA deck, PE core, super flexible... by the end it was so waterlogged no matter where I squeezed it water would shoot out of holes, it must've weighed 20lbs." He was eventually given another Morey Boogie kit board by his friend, on which he learned some of his first manoeuvres including rolls, carves and helicopters.

With a friend's father a commercial diver, Mike and his buddies could alternate hitchhiking with scoping new lineups from a boat, and the shallow break Rockpiles soon becoming the go-to spot. "I didn't really like the surfboard as it just wasn't anywhere near as functional," he said. "As I came to explore hollower waves, bodyboarding made more sense... if I'd grown up in Malibu it probably would have been a totally different deal." One day when Mike was 11 he paddled his kit board out at Rockpiles only to get caught in a rapidly increasing swell, swiftly reaching 6-8ft Hawaiian. "I remember totally freaking out, bailing my board, going underwater and having to swim out and wait for rescue by my older brother," Mike said. "It was the biggest surf I'd ever encountered, and there were no leashes back then."

At 13 Mike's family moved to the Big Island. Now tackling some of the better spots off Kailua-Kona, he impressed a certain Tom Morey in the waves one day, and subsequently chased him for a job at his unit. "It was like full-on Willy Wonka, kid in a candy store," Mike said. "The place was like an R&D centre, just creating stuff, it was awesome... I started cleaning up, but as my relationship with Tom grew I worked up to be able to

work in the main bit and make a few boards and swimfins, it was incredible." During his teens Mike's bodyboarding began to blossom in the punchier waves of Airport and neighbouring reefs on the west side of the Big Island. Although there were growing pockets of bodyboarders on the island at this time – including a young Shane Dorian – Mike mainly surfed by himself or with local surfers who inspired him to push his limits. Around the time Pat Caldwell landed his first el rollo at Sandy Beach, Mike too had begun experimenting in Kona by using the lip to launch him into larger-radius rolls, roll take-offs and early roll-to-helicopters.

At 16 years old Mike began to realise the importance of getting to grips with the Banzai Pipeline. "I knew I had to commit to the wave and learn everything about it," he said. "The first time I surfed it was on a completely different level

MIKE SEARLE

to anything I'd previously experienced." Conditions were 8-10ft Hawaiian, and Mike paddled out with apprehension to sit in the channel and soak up the heavy atmosphere. "It was crowded, guys were yelling at each other, it was a whole new level of intensity, for me it was like surfing Jaws or something," he said. "Not to mention the wave looked like it defied gravity the way it was throwing out, I had no idea what I was dealing with." Mike gradually began edging closer to the peak, and finally got himself in position for one. Paddling for it, he noticed a bunch of surfers also paddling for it inside him, and fearful of someone dropping in on him, he pulled back. That was the end of it; he was no longer given a look in. After an hour he moved across to the peak even further, and was

eventually gifted a messy, junk one with too much west in it. Although far from a classic ride, a symbiotic relationship had been born. It wasn't long though before Mike paid his dues and had his first taste of Pipeline's power from the wrong side of the trench. "I got caught inside and tried to duckdive," he said. "My friend later told me most people didn't do that there, they just ditched their boards instead... I could see why, it didn't work out too well."

Mike missed the first professional bodyboarding competition at Pipeline - the Surecraft Coca-cola Bodyboarding Championships in 1980- as he was never told the event was taking place. "I was so bummed when I heard it had happened without me," he said. "I made sure I was in the next one." In 1982 Mike missed his high school graduation to fly to Oahu to stay with his grandfather and enter his first bodyboard competition at Sandy Beach at 18 years of age. In 3ft Halona Point he finished third, but also began a decade-long rivalry with a young Ben Severson by colliding with him and forcing an interference. Buoyed by a top-three finish behind Pat Caldwell and Jack 'Da Rippa' Lindholm, he returned the next month where he progressed to second, and the following month again, when he claimed his first victory at the third time of asking. This success gave Mike the confidence he needed to return to Oahu over the following few months to compete at the trials ahead of the highly anticipated International Morey Boogie Bodyboard Pro Championships in December. "With guys like JP, Pat, Ben and Jack all living on Oahu, it was easily the most progressive of the islands," Mike said. "Compared to

*"As I came to explore hollower waves, bodyboarding made more sense... if I'd grown up in Malibu it probably would have been a totally different deal."*

the empty places where I surfed at home, Sandy Beach was like a carnival... it was a little Mecca, a full-on scene." This was the breakthrough period. For the next few years – more than a dozen consecutive contests – Mike never once failed to reach a final.

The period was an experiment in cross-pollination, with various styles, moves and skill sets all being brought to the table. "I didn't believe in spinners at the time, I thought they were weak and lame," Mike said. "But after that first competition I realised I needed to learn them if I was to compete, as most of my moves were based on hard turns and carves." However, despite having to learn the threesixty, the ace up Mike's sleeve was his trademark larger-radius roll.

BRIAN BIELMANN

TOM BOYLE

TOM BOYLE

Above: **Classic turbo-charged turn, late 1980s.**

Top: **Shot at G-Land for an O'Neill ad, 1985.**
Above: **Scooping macking Pipeline, March 1983**

Where most riders would simply rise to the top of the wave and flop a quick corkscrew roll before dropping down the face, Mike utilised the natural power and shape of the wave to project and launch from the lip – a technique which was to form the very basis of high-performance aerial bodyboarding.

As 1982 drew to a close, all eyes turned to the inaugural Morey championships at Pipeline. With only six months of contest experience behind him, Mike reached the final but was pipped by the DK wizard Jack Lindholm and Daniel Kaimi. Already an early innovator with airs, half-inverts and the projected roll, the following year Mike began thinking of new moves, coming up with the cutback spinner in California, landing the first air forward at Sunset, and experimenting with combination-axis manoeuvres (which would eventually become the gyroll). "I have always been ambitious with new moves," he said. "But I never liked landing backwards, they've always needed to be functional for me, landing in the direction to continue riding... everyone got something from someone

else at that time though, a spin here, a roll there, that's how it progressed, everyone was a contributor." On 27 July,, 1983, Mike went on a date with bodyboarder Lisa Miller – the only girl to compete at the inaugural world championships – and the pair clicked, staying together from then on and eventually marrying in 1996.

That summer Mike joined the Morey team, and moved to California to be involved with its promotional jamboree series. It didn't start too well. The night before his first jamboree, he and roommate Keith Sasaki scoffed a couple of burritos for dinner, only to discover the next morning they weren't too good. On the long drive through Los Angeles up the coast to Santa Barbara, they needed to make several unscheduled stops. "When we finally hit the beach I ran straight to the bathroom, it was horrendous," Mike said. "Anyway, I recovered and was trying to make a good first impression with the people and the team, but when I was teaching in the water things started gurgling again, I had to run back to the bathroom, burst in,

drop my wetsuit and just let it rip. Whilst I was in there the cleaning guy came in and I could hear him shout: 'Oh Jesus Christ!! Why would someone do this?!?!'... that was my first gig with Morey."

That season he returned to the North Shore and won both the Morey and Scott Hawaii events at Pipeline, earning $9,000 in the process – even more than Triple Crown winning surfer Michael Ho. After his second year of college at the University of Southern California, he moved to Taiwan for a few months to start his own board company, experimenting with EVA foams and beaded polypropylene, a foam core which would eventually become industry-standard. However, despite his diligence and wish to explore EVA's capabilities, he wasn't able to extract any workable products from it and he returned to Oahu shortly after his 21st birthday. He timed it perfectly. With the professional scene about to take off with increased media presence, clever marketing and growing sponsorship, he was in the right place at the right time, with the skills to

Mike spinning in the pocket at G-Land, June 1989.

make it happen. His career opened up like a big Pipe barrel.

Soon sponsored by Scott Hawaii for $75 a month, Mike's sponsorship bandwagon swelled from Pacific Vibrations Surf Shop and Town & Country to soon include the international heavyweights of O'Neill and Gotcha Sportswear, and later Morey and Turbo. In perfect stride, he began winning... virtually everything. Claiming his first world title in 1983, Mike retained his crown in 1984 and again in 1987, 1988, 1989, 1990, 1991, 1992 and 1994. In addition to claiming multiple national, PSAA and Pipeline titles, he also competed in bodysurfing events, eventually winning 13 Pipeline championships. He was the surf media darling; good looking, tanned and athletic, the godfather of bodyboarding with a style the world craved to emulate. He stood apart from other bodyboarders and the surfing community by playing with Pipeline like it was the easiest wave in the world, casually pulling into heavy blue tubes and boosting huge trademark rolls for hundreds of adoring photographers. With Morey's global distribution

> *"It got pretty nuts when there were no barriers between me and the people, they were pushing posters in my face for signatures and I couldn't even see, I got quite phobic of crowds at that point…it was full on, like being a rock star."*

network and Pipeline events televised, he even received fan mail from supporters in one landlocked African nation. He was the king, and his bankability grew accordingly – by the late 1980s he was earning close to $300,000 a year.

In 1986 he was on a PSAA tour trip to Tahiti with Ben Severson and Chris Tennberg when the trio stumbled across a heaving spit at the now famed 'end of the road'. As it happens Mike had actually scoped the spot on a trip the previous year, but hadn't yet joined the dots. The following day he and Chris

rented a Zodiac to explore some new reefs, and on their way home rounded the island and came across the wave from the back – peeling 4-6ft barrels and looking as perfect as anything they could imagine… Teahupo'o's cat was out of the bag. A few years later Mike headed back to Tahiti to coincide with a big south swell that was due to light up Teahupo'o on a whole new level. "When I arrived it was big and it was rising," he said. "When I got out there it was pretty massive." Mike paddled out across the lagoon by himself, but it was only when he got

up close he realised exactly what he was dealing with. As he approached the deepwater channel adjacent to the impact zone a huge wave discharged, creating a spit so ferocious he had to duckdive the explosion of droplets even from the channel. The swell was from the south, a good direction for Teahupo'o, and peaking at 15-18ft in long, glassy walls. "The waves were so ridiculous I laughed out loud," he said. "I was wishing someone else could have been seeing what I was seeing, I shouted 'Oh my god you have got to be kidding me!'"

Working his way into position down the reef, it still took him six or seven attempts to catch one. "It was the first time I'd experienced surf so heavy that as soon as you saw a building wave you had to paddle in as fast as you could, fighting your instincts," he said. "Usually you see a set wave you paddle out to it, but here I was having to get my head down and stroke in just to have a chance of catching it... all my years of surfing Pipe came in handy though, the swell would have been at Second Reef if it'd been breaking there." Mike finally got frustrated and moved in further to negotiate the takeoff's seemingly endless fight against gravity, and eventually caught a couple. "Once you'd dropped in it took a long time to reach the bottom of the wave," he said. "But once you'd bottom turned it just went so glassy... and at that size the waves weren't spitting, they were barfing."

In 1987 Mike moved to Long Beach, California, to relocate closer to the mainland's bodyboarding industry and PSAA tour events. By this stage he had the highest profile in the sport and was hot property, travelling on dozens of promo tours around the world. "My first time in the Canary Islands there were guys following me around by bike and hanging around outside the hotel room," he said. "It got pretty nuts when there were no barriers between me and the people, they were pushing posters in my face for signatures and I couldn't even see, I got quite phobic of crowds at that point... it was full on, like being a rockstar." By this stage Mike had appeared

on the cover of *Surfer* and *Surfing*, and was voted as the best rider at Pipeline by respected stand-up Jon Damm in a poll of the world's best surfers. Even feared North Shore local Johnny Boy Gomes named him in his top ten. Mike was the face of the sport, appearing on global advertisements and earning respect and notoriety by excelling in big waves on the North Shore each winter. In the eyes of many he had made bodyboarding legitimate; but while some surf companies lapped up his exposure, others baulked at offering him a salary close to those of their stand-up riders – even those much less successful.

An example of this prejudice came when he was invited to a tube riding contest at Tavarua, Fiji. Set up by Gotcha's Mark Price, Mike joined expert tube riding surfers such as Tom Curren, Shawn Briley and Shaun Tomson, but his inclusion ruffled feathers. "Claw (Rip Curl founder Doug Warbrick) said to Mark 'Why are you including Mike? You're just setting up a surfer to lose, and what's that going to say about surfing?'" Mike said. "That was a decision moment for me, I realised then these surfers weren't into universal wave riding at all, it was just all about image... it was

lame, but at least it was gratifying to know they didn't even want to play, as they'd get smoked." The situation didn't sit well with Mike, and after failing to negotiate terms with Billabong and Quiksilver, he began to rally for bodyboarders to avoid surf clothing brands, who he felt weren't putting enough back into the sport. "Surf companies were a huge help to us in the early days, but I think I was optimistic to think they would want to get behind bodyboarding further... I feel bad as I take a lot of the responsibility that they stopped doing it," Mike says of his Hawaiian-style stance to hold out for better contracts. "I felt they gave us a shot and I blew it for everyone... if I had handled it differently I think it would have been better for bodyboarding overall, it's something I still carry with me."

Multiple world, national, PSAA and Pipeline champion, Mike had dominated the competition scene throughout the previous decade, but by the early 1990s was looking in new directions to challenge himself. The answer lay beyond the famed breaks of the North Shore, quite literally: the outer reefs. He began his conquest of the North Shore's big-wave spots in an era before jet skis, often paddling out from the beaches for more than a kilometre to tackle giant waves on distant reefs by himself. When jet skis first brought the advent of tow-in surfing, he and big wave specialist Brock Little shunned small wave practice to learn the art directly in 20ft conditions, to mixed success. "One day early on we got caught by a big set and Brock got smoked," Mike said. "It took us almost 40 minutes to get our stuff, outside was 20ft and the inside was like 4-6ft, we lost our boards and kept getting blasted trying to grab them, people were probably calling the coastguard... it was hilarious." Over the next 20 years Mike further explored the North Shore's outer reef

**Far left:** Still competing on the world tour, Mike poses with his family after surfing in the final of the 2012 IBA Pipeline Challenge.
**Left:** With nine world titles by the age of 31, the podiom had become Mike's throne.
**Right:** Cloudbreak lip launch, late 1990s.

frontier, and bodyboarded more than a dozen of its big wave spots, including Maui's notorious Jaws on 2 February, 1996.

The day didn't start well for Mike, who was meant to be on his way to LA for a photoshoot. After three hours sleep he missed his 6am first-class flight and had to get an airport car lot attendant to break into his car with a coat hanger to retrieve his keys. Driving back to the North Shore for a consolation surf, he took a call from movie director Tom Stern. Before he knew it he was on a Maui-bound flight with Brock to tow-in at the most respected big-wave spot in the world - Jaws.

Standing up and feathering in a stiff offshore breeze funnelled from the Peahi valley, a 25ft mountain hollowed out and spat a cloud, half a kilometre out to sea. Mike arrived amped, but despite the fact he was trained, fit and conditioned for big waves – even towing big outer reef North Shore the day before – none of the jet ski crew wanted to give him a shot on his bodyboard, and he remained on the dock. "I felt I was as capable as anyone to surf that place," he said. "But no one wanted to pick me up or take me... I felt like the odd man out, I guess none of them knew what bodyboards were capable of."

After a long wait, Rush Randle eventually swung by and offered Mike the chance to tow into a couple of 20-footers, settling his nerves and showing Laird Hamilton and the other tow-in surfers that he knew what he was doing. Cautiously increasing his rhythm in Peahi's unridden realm, halfway

through the session he switched to another ski and was soon whipped into one of the waves of the day. "It was a bigger scale... a whole 'nother dimension," Mike said of the wave that pitched top-to-bottom in a 25ft bowl. "I came flying into it and hit some chop coming down the face, went up into the air and tried to control it, hit again and went higher, then controlled myself and angled into it a bit more... I almost died. When the lip comes down it's big, but when the barrel starts to pitch out it's really huge." It was the first time a bodyboarder had towed into massive Jaws, redefining what was previously thought possible. By the end of the session he was even punting forward spins on takeoff, much to the amazement of the waiting surfers.

Exactly one month to the day later, Mike and girlfriend of 12 years Lisa Miller were married at the Central Union Church in Honolulu. Bodyboarders such as Tom Boyle, Kainoa McGee, Erin Kamano, Seamus Mercado, Danny and Chris Ann Kim, Ben Severson, JP Patterson and Jack Lindholm all celebrated the day with them, plus Tom Morey, who joined Mike's parents when the congregation was asked to 'Stand up if you've helped raise Mike'.

Four months later and Mike was in Tahiti, surfing solid waves between GOB events. Eventually the swell dwindled, and on 13 July he called Sean Collins at Wave Trak, America's biggest surf forecaster, to get an update. The news was big,

very big. The lull wouldn't last for long – a 25ft-plus swell was due to strike Tahiti in five days, and it looked like it would be all-time. Mike began to think about the possibility of surfing the same swell in Hawaii if he could leave on the 20th to get back in time, and chose to hang around to see how big this hyped swell would turn out to be. On 16 July Sean had recorded 45ft open-ocean seas, and by the following day small islands south of Tahiti were being deluged under gigantic waves. Mike tripped back from an outer island after the swell maxed out to find the main island cranking. "It was absolutely massive and washing under the house," Mike said. "The next day it was total chaos everywhere, we went out to surf Teahupo'o and it was south, massive, fun, and no one out... it was pitting and blowing it guts out."

That night he flew to Honolulu and headed straight for the North Shore to rest for a few hours and prepare for the fanning swell lines to strike Hawaii from the south east. By 3pm the early period was up to 25 seconds and there were murmurings that the largely dormant break Maalaea might start to light up on Maui's west side. In the 1970s it had developed a reputation as the fastest wave in the world, but such was its rarity Mike had yet to experience its freight-train barrels. At 3.30pm Sean confirmed Maalaea would break, but also floated the possibility that since Mike was due in California in the following days anyway, he could theoretically chase the same

swell from there all the way to Alaska – 8,000 miles of travel later. Mike called JP Patterson at Morey to check if he was keen, and the answer was a resounding yes.

By 7.30am the following morning Mike had landed on Maui and driven to Maalaea Beach Park to be greeted with a mechanically perfect 6-8ft right hander screaming down the line, looking like Indonesia. "I'd always wanted to surf it but had no idea where the lineup was," Mike said. "It took quite a while to figure it out, there were bad vibes in the water, it was crowded, fights were going on, but I found a better takeoff zone mid way down... the wave was a hollow, high-speed, big-move setup and you could race in and out of hollow bowls with surplus speed and vert sections perfect for launching." He surfed for seven hours but had no time to rest – the swell was already showing up on Californian buoys, and would peak

the following afternoon. By 7pm he was back on Oahu's North Shore and four hours later on a plane to California.

Early the next morning, 23 July, Mike touched down on LA tarmac and within an hour and a half was out of his hire car and suiting up at the demonic Newport Wedge. "It was as big as I've ever seen it," Mike said. "It was bombing, absolutely humungous, I'd only seen the Wedge break as far out on one other swell, and that was the early 1980s." Mental 25-30ft faces wedged skyward and exploded down the unforgiving sandbank, mainly closing out. Mike paddled out and experienced the carnage for a couple of hours before being ordered out of the water by the lifeguards. Confirming plans with old friend Mike Greenwell, that night the pair jumped aboard his boat and headed up to Central California to score some lesser-known breaks they'd figured would be working.

By the following afternoon they had arrived to see conditions reaching 8ft and thundering hollow down a remote beach in cold water. Several hours and numerous barrels later Mike was physically drained and mentally exhausted, but had started to notice a recognisable rhythm and pattern to the swell. "It dawned on me it had a fingerprint to it," he said. "The way the sets came, it was distinct and unique... there was a little variation in the frequency of the swells from spot to spot, almost like a mood change, but for the most part you could sense the similarity. As strange as it sounds, the swell had taken on a personality of its own."

At 7.30am, 27 July, JP and Mike flew to Anchorage, Alaska, for the final leg of the epic journey. After a connection the pair arrived at the small town of Yukutat, and from there grabbed a single-prop air taxi to wherever they wanted to go. Spotting

a potential rivermouth break 15 minutes later, the pilot duly dipped the plane, swung around and landed them directly on the sand. Surrounded by snow-capped mountains and pine trees, Mike and JP suited up and braved the Alaskan waters to catch the tail end of the swell, still peeling at 3-4ft. "It was coming in the same sequence of sets, and it was amazing to sit in the lineup and know where this huge amount of energy had come from," Mike said. "Finishing the trip was a euphoric feeling, I'd ridden the same storm across the entire Pacific and this was where the swell's energy finally expired."

Mike's efforts over the previous eight days had gathered worldwide coverage, and he even appeared on the front cover of the LA Times with athlete Michael Johnson. "That swell chase was something I'd dreamed of doing, but as it's so expensive it's normally completely out of the realm of reality," he said. "Thankfully I was at a point in my career where I had a virtually unlimited travel budget." The next day, two fishermen were overheard talking in a Yukutat bar about a porpoise they'd spotted doing spins and flips in the waves – unbeknownst to them, it had a blue board and a Hawaiian tan.

In 1994 Mattel, Inc. bought Kransco and took over Morey Boogie. With his signature model selling at a rate of 20,000 units per year, Mike signed up to a new five-year deal, but

said. "It totally killed the sport... surf shops were bummed, they'd bought new boards for $80 to $100 but now you could buy the same boards for $25 at Costco or Walmart, it burned everyone." Over the next couple of years Mike endured a difficult period, going back to basics and focusing on his own company, Mike Stewart Inc, solidifying his future.

In 1999, the first-ever bodyboarding computer game Mike Stewart's Pro Bodyboarding was released for Windows. Boasting twelve types of tricks at eight different breaks and rendered in 3D, the game received positive reviews, with Gaming Entertainment Monthly giving it an 85/100 and GameBlitz 80/100, saying: "This game is a lot of fun, and while arcadey, offers something completely different."

Midway through November 1999, Morey dropped its 17-year support of the Pipeline competition, and with just over

"The next day it was total chaos everywhere, we went out to surf Teahupo'o and it was south, massive, fun, and no one out...It was pitting and blowing its guts out."

Mattel faltered after two, and he entered a messy legal wrangle. Juggling a new house and a high mortgage, Mike suddenly found himself saddled with mounting costs and huge debt, and with poor vested advice and legal bills exceeding $200,000, was left close to bankruptcy. "It was the most expensive university I ever went to," Mike said. "I thought I was secure with them in my contract, I mean Mattel was a multi-billion dollar company at the time, four times bigger than the entire surf industry... but against me it was a sledgehammer versus a mosquito." Mattel went on to offload warehouses full of boards, which ended up on sale at ludicrously low prices at giant retailers. "They were supposed to destroy them as part of our settlement agreement, but they dumped them," Mike

a month left to fund and organise it, Mike stepped in to save the prestigious event. It cost the 11-times Pipeline champion $20,000 to hold the first international competition of the millennium, but he continued to back the event over the following two years under his new company, Mike Stewart Science. Keen to help steer international bodyboarding competitions away from mushy GOB grovel to bigger, heavier waves, Mike also sponsored the 2000 Shark Island Challenge in Australia, going on to win the event in slabbing 4-8ft conditions. In April of that year he was voted as one of the top eight wave riders by *Surfer magazine*, which also went on to recognise him as one of the top 50 most influential surfers of all time.

During this time Harry Antipala had suggested to Mike that it might be a good idea if he removed himself from the voting of Riptide magazine's annual Peer Poll, which he had won each year since its inception in 1992. "It made sense to give someone else a crack at it, and for me to go out on top," Mike said. "I had been there for so long it was time for a change." After the votes were counted in 2000, Mike called Ryan Hardy to tell him he was the new number one ranked rider - such was the significance for Ryan, the Australian got off the phone shaking. "It was so special for me to be able to experience that," Mike said. "Though I'm sure he would have got it that year regardless of whether I was there or not." Ryan went on to dominate the poll for years to come.

In 2001 the Shark Island Challenge was set to go down in the biggest swell witnessed in nearly 30 years. Spots no one had ever seen before – or since – were breaking up and down

Left: Signing frenzy on the Puerto Rican leg of the IBA World Tour.
Right: Mike in flight at the IBA Arica Chilean Challenge, 2012.

Australia's East Coast, but Mike remained in Hawaii awaiting the birth of his first child, Kaimana. Daughter Anela followed in 2004, and with new parental responsibility, his outlook to surfing big or dangerous waves changed. "I thought it would actually be best to step it up," Mike said, seemingly counter-intuitively. "From my experience I felt I was safer charging than hesitating halfway through charging." Shortly afterwards, Mike pushed himself slightly too far at Second Reef Pipeline by paddling out with a sprained ankle and his foot taped in position. Swinging around for a bomb, he promptly overcommitted and got worked. "It was pretty nuts, I got gobbled," Mike said. "But I felt I had to go on it, I couldn't let the mental battle get in the way."

During the last 15 years Mike has devoted more time to mentoring talented young riders. Prodigious young bodyboarders such as Mitch Rawlins, Tom Rigby and more recently Tanner McDaniel have all benefited from Mike's personal wisdom and experience, and while this is obviously the case for his team riders, it's a philosophy he feels strongly about in general. "I'm passionate about passing on information to guys who are receptive to it," he says. "It's about raising the bar as much as you can with as many as you can... it's special for me to see it grow." In addition, he feels a good understanding of the base skills – the old school style of clean lines, smooth turns and harnessing the natural power of the wave – are crucial foundations to the explosive aerials of the new school. "It's something I think I really instilled in Mitch

Rawlins," he said. "He has really begun to merge the two, and it's great to see him on his own mission with his own company also, it's inspiring."

From humble living room beginnings 20 years ago, Mike Stewart Science has grown from strength to strength over the last decade to become one of the sport's leading board and equipment companies. Mike's love of design and manufacture is clearly evident in his products, going all the way back to his intricately-moulded helix Gyroll leash. Mike first began sewing and assembling Gyrolls in his house in 1992, having sourced each of its 14 individual parts from specialist vendors. After a couple of years of development, he took his first box of 12 to Jack's Surf & Sport in Newport Beach, California, but was told they wouldn't sell as they were too expensive. "By the time I'd got back to my house they'd already re-ordered," Mike said. "It took off, my buddy and I made a load more and I filled my Toyota 4Runner with them, it was a little phenomenon." The leash was way ahead of its time in terms of its design and manufacture, featuring a shorter, wider coil and load-bearing oval cross section, and it proved to be a bestseller to this day.

In 2009 Mike won the IBA Arica Chilean Challenge at 46 years old, using all his own equipment. "It was a real milestone for me," he said. "Not only to win in my forties, but to be able to do it using all my own gear from my own company... it was really gratifying to be able to sponsor myself and not be reliant on other companies, I'd reached one of my goals."

Mike has enjoyed three decades at the top of the sport, inspiring hundreds of thousands of bodyboarders and experiencing an unparalleled career in scope, success and legacy. His importance and influence are genuinely without measure, and it's fair to say the sport of bodyboarding wouldn't be where it is today without his existence. Yet despite everything, from six-figure salaries and multiple world titles to meeting people who have tattoos of his signature, Mike has remained incredibly humble and never subscribed to the hype and notoriety surrounding him. "It's endemic to bodyboarding, and it's all relative," he says. "I've always kept it in perspective, I go a few hours from the coast and no-one knows me... bodyboarding is one facet of a subculture of a sport that is not in the major limelight."

Nonetheless, Mike feels great pride in his ability to continue to inspire riders as he approaches 50 years old. "I've a good diet and a specific workout routine I follow rigourously," he says. "I may not have the same elasticity and recovery times as I did, but I am now stronger, more flexible and in better shape than I was when I was 18. I hope I've shown that bodyboarding isn't as age-restricted as people might have thought it was, and I still have some things to contribute... age is just a number."

After dropping out of the top 24 at the end of 2011, Mike fired back in February 2012 by finishing second in flawless 6-8ft Pipeline, setting himself up for a comeback season to requalify and chase the world title once more in 2013 – an incredible 31 years after he first started. "Tom Morey's vision was to get more people to enjoy the ocean, and if I can help be the purveyor of this, then awesome," Mike says with a chuckle. "I'm stoked to have encouraged people to embrace what they want in their heart, and to enjoy the ocean on a bodyboard... it's so much fun."

"I may not have the same elasticity and recovery times as I did, but I am now stronger, more flexible and in better shape than I was when I was 18. I hope I've shown that bodyboarding isn't as age-restricted as people might have thought it was, and I still have some things to contribute... age is just a number."

Mariana Nogueira at the 1998 Morey Pipeline contest.

# The Women

Right from the earliest days of the sport female bodyboarders have charged hard. Following the Brazilian boom of the 1980s, female competitions exploded in popularity in the 1990s, backed by strong Japanese sponsorship. Today women's bodyboarding remains extremely popular, and continues to grow around the world.

Neymara Carvalho on the North Shore in the mid 1990s.    Neymara claims the Pipeline Pro, 2011.    Mariana Nogueira.    Stephanie Pettersen.

**From disparate beginnings, women's bodyboarding grew steadily throughout the 1980s, principally in Brazil, where for a while it was more popular than male bodyboarding.** From having to originally compete against men in competition, women riders first vied in their own all-female championship at Pipeline in 1990, and with a lot of hard work and determination, their own division of the Global Organisation of Bodyboarding (GOB) World Tour in 1995. With annual Pipeline competitions and multiple tour stops around the world, women's bodyboarding grew rapidly throughout the 1990s, especially in places such as Japan. Following the formation of the International Bodyboard Association (IBA) in 2004, women's bodyboarding has enjoyed mixed success but remained a firm fixture on the calendar, and today the Women's World Tour (WWT) is solidified, respected and heading in the right direction.

Women's participation in the new sport of bodyboarding grew in Hawaii in the late 1970s, with stars like Phyllis

Dameron carving the track for both female and big-wave riders alike. Phyllis began bodyboarding in 1975, paddling out by herself at 12ft Sandy Beach. She soon graduated to the North Shore and developed a reputation as a big wave charger, outdoing the men by surfing notorious spots like Sunset and Waimea in maxing conditions, usually spotted bouncing down giant faces with a delicate finesse.

As the 1980s boogied on, so did the female participation in Hawaii, but it was Brazil where women's involvement in the sport was taking off. With a wildly popular and well developed national tour, the women enjoyed much greater exposure than the men, who had to fight hard to get coverage in the media. "The level was pretty high," six-time Brazilian men's champion Guilherme Tamega said. "The girls always had prettier moves in the small surf, it just looked better watching them ride than the boys, so the biggest picture in the newspaper was always the girls." As the Brazilian contest scene was booming, things were also moving in Hawaii,

with riders such as Chris Anne Kim and Shawnee Oide pushing the sport forward, both in the water and on land. As well as top competitors, the pair later helped set up the Hawaiian Association of Women Bodyboarders, organised contests at Pipeline, gave talks in schools and promoted girl's bodyboarding on the Hawaiian news channel KHON.

In 1987 the talented young Brazilian rider Glenda Kozlowski travelled to Sandy Beach, Oahu, and won the amateur world championship title, backing it up the next year by winning the women's open division of the US Nationals at Oceanside, California, at just 14 years of age. Seeing Brenda surf at Sandy Beach was a wake-up call for Chris Anne Kim and the Hawaiian girls: "Following that competition we thought, 'Whoa, okay, there are other girls out there' and we started pushing ourselves," she said. "It pretty much changed everything in our mind of having more contests and getting more exposure through the magazines. It was time to step it up." The year after Glenda's success she was joined by a

Daniela Freitas goes for broke at the 1998 Pipe Championships.

group of her Brazilian peers, who dominated the various age groups and retained the title, won by top domestic champion Mariana Nogueira.

The next year the Brazilian girls travelled to Australia and California, competing against the men and even defeating riders such as Jay Reale and Guilherme Tamega. At Pipeline, women riders Leila Ali, Daniela Freitas, Stephanie Pettersen and Claudia Ferrari all faced men in competition, but in 1989 the Association of Women Bodyboarders was formed, and things started to turn a corner. A non-profit organisation founded to promote the sport and help in its pursuit of 'excellence, fairness and safety in competition and recreation', the association grew to have representatives in Australia, Brazil, Chile, Hawaii, Ireland, Japan, Peru, Portugal, Puerto Rico and the United States.

In 1990 the first world championship of women's bodyboarding was held at Pipeline, promoted by Bob Thomas. Four of the top five riders were Brazilian, with Stephanie Pettersen taking the title and a cheque for a modest $200.

The following year the event was sponsored by Laguna Sportswear, and with increasing domination the top six riders were all Brazilian. By 1994 the prize purse had reached $10,000, with $1,100 for first place, rising to $3,500 the next year, and a $20,000 prize purse offering $5,000 for first place the year after. Women's bodyboarding had taken off, and in 1995 it graduated from a one-off Pipeline event to join the men on the newly formed GOB World Tour. Despite talented Hawaiian riders such as Shawnee Oide, Chris Anne Kim and the influential Carol Philips all representing the islands in this period, it was the Brazilian riders who commanded the sport with Mariana and Isabel Noguiera, Stephanie Pettersen,

Claudia Ferrari, Daniela Freitas, Neymara Carvalho, Karla Costa, Soraia Rocha and Claudia Santos all finishing strongly.

By the mid 1990s women's bodyboarding was growing exponentially in Japan, and with regular features and exposure in the bodyboard magazine *Flipper*, the majority of top riders sported Japanese stickers. "At one stage I had seven Japanese sponsors," Stephanie Pettersen remembers. "People were just calling me asking to sponsor me, I didn't even have to try… every single one of them was from Japan." By 1996 Casio Baby-G had come on board to sponsor the X-Press World Championship of Women's Bodyboarding, and top female riders were becoming well supported. Daniela Freitas was

Left: The Pipe Championships have long provided a coming together of the worldwide bodyboarding sisterhood, this is from the late 1990s.
Below: Big-wave pioneer Phyllis Damerson poses for a profile.

sponsored by American Airlines and giant Brazilian soccer club Flamengo, while Stephanie Pettersen rode for Baby-G, which alongside other deals earned her $50,000 per year. Of all the countries on the WWT however, international women bodyboarders were most revered in Japan, even appearing on the covers of the nation's fashion magazines. "We actually had to hide in the bathroom to not be attacked by girl fans at contests," Stephanie said. "It was crazy... we were like superstars over there."

Women's bodyboarding suffered a dip towards the end of the decade however, and with poor waves and a faltering Japanese economy, support and sponsorship slowed. Then in 2000 the women showed they could handle the heavy stuff at a GOB expression session ahead of the infamous Tahiti Skins Event, won by Stephanie Pettersen in 6ft conditions at the feared Teahupo'o. The following year she backed up her victory with second and first-place finishes at the double Pipeline events – the Mike Stewart Science Pipeline Pro and V-Bodyboards World Championship of Women's Bodyboarding

respectively. Stephanie was crowned world champion for a record fourth time in 2002, and she began the following season by topping Pipeline's podium once more. However, her dream start was soon stopped dead in its tracks. Not able to secure sponsorship, she was unable to travel to Portugal in August to continue her hunt for a fifth world title, and quit the sport citing a lack of support.

In the following years magazine coverage of women's bodyboarding began to dry up, but the WWT fought on with new riders such as Japan's Aoi Koike and Moe Watanabe, Australia's Kira Llewellyn and Mandy Zieren, and French champion Heloise Bourroux all in the race for world titles. As the freshly rebranded IBA gradually found its feet under Terry McKenna's leadership, so the women's tour became a firmer fixture, and with a growing wave of international riders such as Portugal's Rita Pires, Puerto Rico's Natasha Sagardia and Spain's Eunate Aguirre all competing, the WWT had a renewed focus and greater responsibility.

In 2010 IBA Pty Ltd bought the rights for the WWT, and

alongside the new Grand Slam Series (GSS), Global Qualifying Series (GQS) and Dropknee World Tour (DKWT) for men, it steadily increased its coverage and exposure in its own grand slam events. Leading a new movement of progressive riders, Brazilian champion Isabela Sousa took her first world title in 2010 and finished second behind an in-form Eunate Aguirre in 2011. After a four-way battle in the first part of the 2012 season, Isabela quickly dominated the rest of the tour, wrapping up her second world title by September and returning home to a public parade, a raft of media, and a state reception with the Secretary for Sports.

For a great many years women's bodyboarding fought hard to be independently recognised on the international scene alongside men, and despite facing many uphill battles in recent times - both in sponsorship and coverage – it has cemented a strong world tour with a global following. Given the chance, today's WWT can greatly augment popularity within the sport, and provide a healthy platform for future generations of female professional bodyboarders.

# Michael Eppelstun
## *The Innovator*

Michael 'Eppo' Eppelstun burst on to the world scene in the early 1990s, changing the sport's direction forever. Australia's first world champion in 1993, Eppo sent bodyboarding skyward, inspiring future generations and creating the most advanced manoeuvres the sport had ever seen – the double roll, the air roll spin (ARS) and the backflip. His gymnastic style and gutsy approach to the North Shore quickly elevated him from a comparative nobody to the hottest name in the sport, and paved the way for aspiring future Australian world champions. Eppo's legacy lives on with each big boost and avant-garde aerial seen today, all underpinned by a healthy dose of fun.

**Born on the last day of 1970, Eppo grew up in the country town of Cowra, four hours west of Sydney.** Before moving to Port Macquarie at 12, Eppo had only ever seen the ocean twice – once at 7 years old, the other at 9, when he enjoyed riding waves on an inflatable air mattress. Arriving in Port Macquarie in October, 1983, he was quickly exposed to the budding movement of bodyboarding, and immediately sought a board for Christmas that year. "I remember my dad pointing to a $15 yellow foam board and saying 'Santa might bring you that mate', and I said 'I don't think so, if you get me that it's

going in the bin! I want that $69 WTS one with the glued on fins'." Santa duly came around to his wish, and with his new WTS board Eppo was hooked, even after knocking his prized fins out first session by riding it up onto the beach.

The first day back in school after the summer, Eppo was sat in a class next to David 'Goose' Gosby. The pair clicked and as new best mates became inseparable; bodyboarding, hanging out and going to the beach every day. As groms, Eppo and Goose's main inspiration was Port Macquarie local Rob Cotter, who had big sponsors, competed nationally and had the best tube style in the business. Despite learning a lot from Rob, Eppo cared less about method and just wanted to do as many things as he could. "I was an ugly rider, but an aggressive rider," he said. "I just wanted my riding to be explosive and exciting... I never claimed to be pretty doing it." Eppo's attentions soon grew to include Rob's contemporaries, namely Shark Island ripper Ross 'Hellman' Hawke and North Narrabeen's Dave Appleby – who later mentored him in how to be a professional bodyboarder in everything from negotiating sponsors' contracts to how to greet kids at promos.

There was still no competition scene in Port Macquarie by mid 1987, but on 14 June an event was held at Middle Rock by the Bonny Hills Boardriders, and a frothing 16-year-old Eppo took it out – beating none other than his hero Rob Cotter in the process. Following the success of that contest Eppo's father John Eppelstun wholeheartedly backed his son's new passion, and called a meeting in September to discuss the formation of a local bodyboard club. More than 200 members of the public attended the gathering, and the Hastings Bodyboard

Club was born. Competitions were run on the first weekend of every month, and after three straight victories Eppo was declared the open winner of the Port Macquarie area. The following year it took off, and more than 80 local kids signed up as members. In 1989 the club graduated to become the Port Macquarie Bodyboard Association, boasting a number of established and up-and-coming rippers who took out contests, appeared across the pages of new magazine *Riptide* and busted out in the latest videos – these included Rob Cotter, Goose, Peter and Vicki Gleeson, Ashley and Adam Murray, Simon and Patrick Navin, Simon Andrews, Luke Berhmann, Stewart Clark, Shane McEwan, Matthew Hay, Wayne Hadfield and Anthony Summers. As the club grew, a new wave of Port riders such as Damian King, Todd DeGraaff, Rick Bannister, Simon Thornton, Steve Sonter, Mason Rose, Luke Hall, Todd Lee, and

Pipeline. 1996. Unmistakably Eppo.

later Chase O'Leary and Sam Bennett all helped Port Macquarie become officially known as the 'Bodyboarding Capital of Australia.'

Now firmly bitten by the contest bug, Eppo followed up his local victories with another win at Lighthouse Beach in the Zone regional titles. In the final he beat prodigy Warrick Appleton, who had taken out the open division of the 1984 Morey Boogie Australian Championships at just 14 years old, and finished second behind Mike Stewart at the 1987 South Pacific Pro-Am. Winning the Zone title also meant Eppo qualified for the state titles in New South Wales, where he was told if he made a final he would get a BZ sponsorship. Buoyed by the notion of a high-profile board sponsor, he battled it out in the junior division to finish third and collected a new BZ Stinger as his first sponsored board. "Unfortunately it was a banana," Eppo said. "I went for one surf on it and brought it back saying I couldn't ride it... they said 'What do you mean you can't ride it?' I said 'I can't ride it, and if I have to ride it then I don't want the sponsorship'." They duly sorted him out an arcel BZ Pro. "It was stiff as shit, and I loved it," he said. "It was as fast as they come and I didn't want to know about PE anymore, I could hit the lip and just fly... but jeez I destroyed them."

In 1990 Eppo travelled to Sydney for the Australian titles at Manly Beach, and in confident fashion quickly progressed through three heats. Reaching the semifinals, he found himself up against three of the best riders Australia had ever produced; Steve 'Bullet' Mackenzie, Ross Hawke and Matt Riley, who by then were cutting their teeth at the infamous Shark Island. "I just turned to my mates and said 'Right, I'm not winning this, let's go and get on it'," Eppo said. They bought a carton of 250ml 'twist-top' VBs and went into Sydney that night to carry on, returning in a haze sometime after 2am. Eppo paddled out the next morning feeling a little worse for wear, but after a couple of good waves and a reverse floater off the lip, he won the heat. "No one had ever seen one before," Eppo said. "Nick White who was commenting on it said it was a 'reverse belly air', but there definitely wasn't any air in it." He went on to finish third in the final in small conditions, behind wave-magnet Bullet and original South Coast pioneer Karl Fjelsted. Gone were the days the flannelette 'country bumpkin' thought tube riding involved rolling around the local BMX track in a tractor tyre – he'd now found his calling.

The same year, Eppo endured an extremely hard time after his best friend Goose died at just 18 years of age. A lifetime sufferer of a congenital heart condition, Goose had had a pacemaker fitted in his early teens and from that point on lived an extremely healthy lifestyle, centred on his love for bodyboarding. On 19 September, 1990, he was surfing at Lighthouse Beach when he drowned after a heart attack in the water. Eppo arrived at the beach to see a shocked Pete Gleeson and an ambulance with Goose inside, but it was too late, he had passed away three weeks shy of his 19th birthday. Eppo struggled to deal with Goose's passing, and in the aftermath spiralled into a depressive period of drinking, before waking up on Anzac Day in a garden with a ripped shirt and one shoe on. "I remember coming to and seeing these Anzacs (Australian and New Zealand Army Corps) looking at me in disgust, wondering what had happened to the youth of today," Eppo said. "I remember walking home really disappointed and ashamed of myself." That day Eppo decided to snap out of it, pull himself together and focus on getting to Hawaii.

Photocopying an entrance form for the world titles he'd borrowed from Ross Hawke, Eppo filled it in and sent it off with the necessary documentation and his entry fee not knowing if he'd get in, but needing the motivation. Turned down by John Holmes at BZ for sponsorship of the trip, Eppo haggled a board and fins to be donated for a raffle to try and raise the money himself. Now with a goal, he and Pete Gleeson organised a live band at the local surf club – raising $800 – and every

Thursday evening and Saturday morning they would sit with a table and chair at nearby shopping centres, drumming up support for 'local bodyboarders going for the world title'. Eppo was working as a pastry chef at this time, and with help from Goose's mother, set up cake stalls on local streets, altogether raising $4,500 to get to Hawaii for the winter of 1990/91. Air tickets covered, the pair arrived on Oahu with $1,000 cash in their hands.

For three solid months before the trip, Eppo had juggled his work and fundraising with fitness training to get ready for his first North Shore experience. Occasionally joined by Pete, Eppo and school mate Marcus Brabant (a future top professional surfer) were trained hard by Marcus' father, Jimbo. In addition to swim training, they undertook sand runs, river paddling, log running, hill running, sit ups, push ups, burpees, and stair runs to finish off the sessions. "He taught us to hold our breath, swim 25 metres underwater, pop up for five seconds and go back under again to swim for another 25 metres," Eppo said."We did this seven times in a row, to simulate taking a seven-wave Hawaiian set on the head." Jimbo went on to do a great deal of filming of Eppo, helping him document his manoeuvres and consistently up his game. "If it wasn't for him I would never have made it," he said.

For the inaugural trip to Hawaii, Maroubra ripper PJ Hyland had hooked Eppo and Pete up with a place to stay at North Shore charger Kainoa McGee's house. After exiting the airport however the pair waited eight hours for him to answer his phone and pick them up. Finally they arrived at the house in Waikiki to find no room, other than the shallow loft space above his garage. "We squeezed up there and went to sleep, then something ran across my face," Eppo said. "Then one ran across my shirt, and my legs, and I thought 'What the f--k is that?!' I turned the light on and there were hundreds, literally hundreds, of giant two-inch long cockroaches up there with us running around, we couldn't get back to sleep for the whole night!" After filling nine cockroach traps full over the next two nights, they hadn't made a dent into the cockroach population of the loft, and yet stayed up there for another week.

Eppo celebrated his 21st birthday in a hotel room in the middle of Waikiki with one of Kainoa's friends who was also celebrating his birthday. The party was insane with fancy cocktails, a bath full of alcohol, and firecrackers being let off in the room, including a massive one which seemed to shake the entire building. Around 20 minutes later the cops arrived in force, running in through the door with guns drawn, shouting for everyone to get down on the ground. A drunken Eppo was thrown against a wall after opening the door and dragged through the corridor. After berating the still 20-year-old Australian that he hadn't yet reached the legal drinking

age ('What!? I've been drinking for three years officer!') the police made everyone empty their drinks and the party was over. Welcome to Hawaii, USA.

Regardless of his hardcore training regime before the trip, Eppo was never all that comfortable in waves over 10ft, and was instead more excited by hitting lips in the 6-8ft range. "It was heaven on a stick having that extra power, and in just being there... I was standing at Beach Park with Seamus (Mercado) on one side, Hauoli Reeves on the other, Mike (Stewart) was sitting looking at Pipe, then Dean Marzol arrived on a pushbike, we couldn't believe it," he said. "I had a photographer come up to me that year asking for a couple of portrait shots to go with some action shots she'd taken of me... I came home to find those photos splashed across Riptide, it blew me away."

Soon enough the big day was upon them and Eppo paddled out at 6-8ft Pipeline for his first heat in the world titles, riding best mate Goose's board. Making a couple of 6ft barrels and progressing through his opening round cleanly, he was knocked out the next heat by Chris Burkhart and finished equal 33rd. For Eppo, however, the experience and general buzz of that trip gave him his first taste of living his

dream, and he knew instantly that was what he wanted to do each year from then on. "I remember seeing Mike Stewart do this massive roll in the final against Kainoa, it was the best thing I had ever seen in my life," he said. "Seeing that in real life triggered something in me."

The sport was booming in Australia during this period with surf companies Billabong, Quiksilver and Rip Curl all packing strong bodyboarding teams. In 1992 Eppo signed with Billabong, and began experimenting with new moves to up his profile, soon landing the double roll. Caught on camera by videographer Chris Stroh, Eppo asked for it be kept secret and not shown to anyone before he went to Hawaii for the 1992/93 winter. This was to be Eppo's season, showcasing his double roll and using the punchy bowls of the North Shore to launch some of the most inspiring aerials the sport had ever seen. Instantly recognisable with his frog-legged style, cameramen snapped so quickly they couldn't change film in time. Eppo capped it off in January by beating Mike Stewart, Guilherme Tamega and Aka Lyman in the Pipeline final to become the first ever Australian world champion.

During the championships Eppo reverse-charge called his sponsor John Holmes after each heat and hassled him for how much extra he would get if he could win the next round. "Once I'd made the semi-finals I called him again and asked how much I'd get if I got to the final," Eppo said. "He told me I'd get a little more than I was on, but if I won the whole thing he'd give me $20,000... I held on to that. After I won the world title I dedicated the win to Goose, crossed the road to call my dad and tell him what I'd done whilst bawling my eyes out, then composed myself to call John Holmes and tell him to cough up."

After returning to Australia things got serious for the out-of-left-field fun-loving country bumpkin, and suddenly he was on the hunt for a manager to make the most of his newfound fame. Three years prior, Eppo had approached sports manager Mike Perry, who at the time had told him he was still a nobody, but to get back in touch if he ever became world champion. Eppo had never forgotten this, and after a tumultuous period after he returned home without successful management,

so he could tell him what he was doing. "As Pete was paddling out I took off on this really nice 3ft one, hit the lip, did this big ARS and landed – bang – facing forward... I carried on and skimmed across to him on the shoulder and his jaw had dropped open. I said 'So what is it? What am I doing?' and he said 'Eps, I don't know what the f--k you're doing... it's like a roll and a flip or something." Eppo called Chris Stroh and said he had better come up as he had something new for him. The following day Chris arrived, and after filming him for the next week had shortened Eppo's description of an 'air, roll, spin' to simply 'ARS'.

Three months later, Eppo was still trying to master Ben Holland's twisted air reverse, and whilst surfing North Wall one day again landed something new. "I went for the section and paused as I didn't know whether to do an ARS or not, but I'd already hit it," he said. "I just kept flying and landed it backwards, falling off... I thought 'Hmmm', paddled right back out, took off on another, hit the lip and went bang, flew, landed backwards and this time spun it around. I knew at that point what I was doing... the backflip." Eppo kept the new move secret and didn't do it again for a further six months, purely to stop it taking away from the glory of his ARS. It

extensively, and in 1994 and 1995 his daughters Bree and Taya were born. The arrival of children meant Eppo soon had to re-evaluate his career, and by mid 1997 had already entertained thoughts of leaving the sport. "It got to a stage where I had to choose between going for another world title and spending time with my family," he said. "I reached a point where I had to ask myself what I wanted from life." In 1999 Eppo retired from the GOB World Tour and travelled around Australia for nine and a half months with Krista, Bree and Taya. Incorporating a promotional tour, Eppo had a page in Riptide each month and filmed 33 instructional segments as he travelled for Billabong Surf TV.

After the trip Eppo had an uncomfortable wake-up call when Billabong's renewed contract tender had been slashed by three-quarters. "I was devastated when I got offered that, after all those years I couldn't believe it," he said. "I wanted to set fire to my clothes in front of their shop I was so angry." Instead, Eppo was given the chance to manage its bodyboarding team on a salary of $32,000 for a three-day week. He snapped it up. With a budget of $185,000, the all-star team included riders such as Damian King, Mitch Rawlins, Andrew Lester, Ryan Hardy, Beau Day and Dave Ballard (Billabong's longest-running sponsored rider). Things were looking good, but during the early 2000s the main Australian surf brands started dropping bodyboarding. In 2005, after failing to convince Billabong to increase its support, Eppo left after being faced with a budget cut by more than $100,000.

*"I just kept flying and landed it backwards, falling off… I thought 'Hmmm', paddled right back out, took off on another, hit the lip and went bang, flew, landed backwards and this time spun it around. I knew at that point what I was doing… the backflip."*

drove five hours to the Gold Coast to remind him of what he had said. Mike turned him down again, but undeterred, Eppo hung around to surf over the coming days and not let the subject drop. "By the fourth day Mike said to me 'You're not f--king leaving are you?' and I told him I was world champion but still surviving on just $75 a week." The pair agreed to a 10 per cent commission, shook hands and the next year Eppo earned $156,000.

In mid 1993 after seeing fellow Australian Ben Holland perform a twisted air reverse – which would also appear on Ballistic, the fourth in the Underground Tapes series – Eppo believed he had seen the future. After visualising a new type of manoeuvre in his head, he paddled out at Lighthouse Beach one day and attempted it five times, landing three of them. He woke excited early the next morning and paddled out again, this time attempting 20 of them and landing 15. "I went 'Nah, this can't be right, they're too easy'," he said. That weekend he invited Pete to surf with him and check out this new move

was an exciting time in the sport's history, two of its most spectacular and important manoeuvres had been created in quick succession, and inspired a whole new generation of riders to get freaky.

In October 1993 Eppo signed with Terry Fleming at Manta, receiving $25,000, a car, fuel voucher, travel allowance and royalties from its Blade fins and his signature model, the Eppo Air. After the Hawaii season, Eppo and partner Krista travelled to California to visit Jay Reale. It was during their stay he received his first faxes detailing his monthly board royalties; which in November, December and January amounted to $12,000, $18,000 and $15,000 respectively. That year he earned $60,000 in royalties from his signature board and additional $20,000 in royalties from Manta's Blade fins. In the following years Eppo focused on becoming the consummate professional, and worked hard on promotion, stoking the coals of the bodyboarding fire.

During the mid 1990s Eppo competed and travelled

At this stage Eppo had moved on to focusing his efforts on his own bodyboard shop, taking it from under his house to a warehouse, and then on to the Old Burleigh Theatre Arcade on the Gold Coast. Business was booming, and following another trip around Australia with Mike Stewart and his family in 2006, Eppo and Krista decided to open a second store in Mooloolaba on the Sunshine Coast. He grew both stores over the following years, but with a deteriorating cash flow situation and mounting debt, was forced to sell his Burleigh store in October, 2008. With $80,000 of debt carried to the Mooloolaba store, and with the world economic crisis by then in full flow, it too folded at the end of 2010. After 14 months of clearing his remaining debts, Eppo's house was flooded after heavy rain in March, 2012, causing more than $150,000 of damage and forcing the family to move to a temporary unit for several months. "Despite what's happened lately I'm pretty happy in life right now... I've still got a house, my wife and two kids and all our health," Eppo says. "There are a lot of people worse off than me."

Right: **North Shore backflip, late 1990s, a sponsor's dream.**

Tamega executes a trademark frog-legged forward spin at Pipeline, 1995.

# Guilherme Tamega

## The Charger

Six-time world champion Guilherme Tamega is bodyboarding's strongest competitor. Renowned for his fierce determination and 'go hard' attitude in big waves, the Brazilian is a national celebrity and has competed at the top of the sport for more than 20 years. Attacking with a unique style, his seemingly fearless approach of busting big moves in the heaviest of conditions has given him a level of respect in the sport reserved for only a very few. GT has dedicated his entire life to bodyboarding, and is the only rider who can match his six world titles with six second-places.

**Born on 3 September 1972, Guilherme Tamega grew up with three older brothers, each separated in age by two years.** Son of a banker father and a travel agent mother, he had a modest upbringing in a three-bedroom apartment on the eighth floor of a building a short walk from the famous Copacabana Beach. Guilherme got along very well with his brothers growing up, but naturally a competitive rivalry soon blossomed, and, as the youngest sibling, he formed a steely determination to beat them at everything, from soccer to swimming. This spirited environment instilled the importance of winning to Guilherme, and as they began pushing one another in the water he started taking on bigger and bigger surf, goading them to outdo him in Copacabana's punishing 8ft shorey. It certainly dealt out some beatings, but

MIKE SEARLE

as his older brothers stood watching, the fact he was tackling it at all gave him his first taste of victory.

At 11 years old, Guilherme followed in his older brother's footsteps and took up stand-up surfing. He bought a board and learned to balance, but within a year he had lost interest, deciding instead to get into BMX riding. Despite finding a new thrill of competing, it wasn't long before he came to the conclusion that the water was where he belonged, and soon ditched his wheels for half a Morey Boogie Aussie which had washed up on the beach. "It had belonged to this local guy," he said. "He was the only guy in the whole area who had a bodyboard, but this one day here it was, on the beach snapped in half lengthways, but at least it gave me the chance to ride a half of it." He paddled it out, and after dropping into a few heavy shorey barrels he decided there and then that bodyboarding would 'be his thing'.

It was April 1985, and with a fresh new Morey Boogie 139 under his arm, Guilherme wasted no time in marking his intentions. Just eight months later (and having already upgraded to the Mach 7-7) the little kid from Rio snagged a second place in a national event at Itacoatiara, gaining him his first sponsor and widespread exposure in the process. It was the start of a career which has supported him ever since – the only job he's ever had is to bodyboard. "I remember surfing that comp with just one fin, a giant scuba diving flipper, on my right foot, with my left foot free," he said. "The idea of fins didn't feel at all natural to me, I much preferred to have my feet free and feel the sand under my toes when I was jumping out of the shorey." Progressing through heats with big looping air rolls on the rights, he soon found himself in the final facing top national amateur Paulo

CHRIS POWER

TUNGSETNN

Esteves. "I was just watching him surf in that final, he didn't let me get any waves, I was just bait," he said. Despite being beaten, Guilherme had received his first proper lesson on how to surf competitively, something which was to become his trademark.

The following year Guilherme began winning events and so started an explosive three-year period of competing before turning professional at 16 years old. When he was 15, the tiny grom travelled to the North Shore of Oahu for a month and scored 10ft Pipeline, much to the amusement of the Hawaiian locals. "These giant locals would paddle past me in disbelief saying 'How old are you!?!' I always looked a lot younger than I was, it was funny," he said. "Still, you don't see many 15-year-olds tackling 10ft Pipe, it was my dream to go there." He returned home to the Brazilian amateur circuit with a major confidence boost, and had made a statement on the biggest

stage there was – those North Shore locals would later come to know him, but furthermore, to respect him.

By 1988 the competition scene in Brazil was huge; events made national television and were supported by international companies such as Blaupunkt and Dow Chemicals. Sponsors' scaffolding towers adorned beaches, television cameras rolled, and as the best amateur rider in Brazil, Guilherme's rise to national champion couldn't have been timed better. "The level of riding in the amateur Brazilian tour events at that time became higher than the professionals," he said. As a young teenager, Guilherme had established a healthy competition rivalry with Marcelo Siqueira. As the pair turned professional together at 16 years old (avoiding a rule change to bump the minimum pro rider age up to 18) they immediately stamped their authority on the new division, knocking out established professionals all over the country and consistently making

finals against one another.

After being crowned the Brazilian amateur champion in 1988, Guilherme became national professional champion in 1989 and 1991. Feeling his time was ready, he returned to Hawaii at 19 years old to compete against a wider field of riders at an international level. In his first event at the Morey Boogie World Championships at Pipeline he made the final, finishing fourth. During the next three years he was repeatedly crowned the Brazilian national champion, and returned each year to Pipeline, finishing third in 1992 and second in 1993. Despite losing to Australian Michael 'Eppo' Eppelstun in the final that year, American bodyboard company Wave Rebel saw potential in the charge-hard youngster and flew to Brazil to offer Guilherme a contract – including his own signature model and the opportunity to move to California to work on his board. He jumped at the chance, signed the dotted line and upped sticks

Far left: **Pipeline foamball roll.**
Left: **Indo boat trip air forward.**
Right: **Think he loves the taste of victory?**

to Oceanside to live with founder of *Bodyboard International Magazine*, Patti Serrano.

Wave Rebel timed its offer perfectly. Returning to Hawaii in 1994 and buoyed by his new contract, the 21-year-old Guilherme won his first world title in some of the biggest Pipeline contest conditions ever, with a deep double barrel and a huge el rollo through a heavy closeout end section. The victory earned Guilherme $6,000 and also started a career-long battle with Mike Stewart, who had dominated the sport internationally in the 1980s, and who showed no intention of slowing down into the 1990s. "Mike was my biggest rival, not only in the water but out of the water too," he said. "I wanted to beat him more than anything… we got along well, but when we went against each other sparks just flew."

Returning to Brazil as world champion, the reception for Guilherme was overwhelming. A new national hero, he became a household name with his performance at Pipeline appearing across all of the national newspapers and television channels – he was even given a Medal of Honor from the city of Rio de Janeiro (in a ceremony that until that point had only been reserved for national soccer treasures Pele and Zito.) "I came home a celebrity, I was huge," he said. "I would walk down the street shaking hands, waving at people, it was incredible… it cemented my name in the sports world of Brazil."

Guilherme went on to win the new Global Organisation of Bodyboarding (GOB) World Tour in 1995, 1996 and 1997, becoming four-times world champion by the age of 25. During this period he travelled continually, competing in

*"Mike was my biggest rival, not only in the water but out of the water too, I wanted to beat him more than anything… we got along well, but when we went against each other sparks just flew."*

multiple tours and hiring personal trainers and dieticians to help keep him in peak physical condition. Becoming American professional champion in 1995, he was also crowned International Surfing Association (ISA) World Surfing Games champion at Huntington Beach in 1996. It was during this hectic period Guilherme once made nine finals in nine consecutive weekends, across the US tour, Brazilian tour and

world tour.

This was the glory era for Guilherme, who by now was earning in the region of $150,000 per year in prize money and riding for Wave Rebel and Redley. He remained undefeated as world champion until 1998 when South African supergrom Andre Botha stole his crown, knocking him off the top spot for the following two seasons. For Guilherme this is still something he remains immensely proud of. "I know some people don't care about second places, but I do," he said. "It's still very hard to be there and get that close to winning, it's still an accomplishment." In 2000 he moved back to Brazil and wasted no time in winning his second ISA world championship title and sixth Brazilian national tour title.

By this time there was growing discontent in the sport; although the GOB was providing a big tour, it had veered away from world-class waves and as a result had lost some of its credibility. After Mike Stewart and several fellow Hawaiians had voiced opposition to the tour, it seemed only a matter of

time before it was overhauled and steered in a new direction. Following the epic Tahiti Skins Event 2000 at Teahupo'o and with tour director Bob Thomas' vision, the Super Tour was formed – with an emphasis on fewer, bigger events at waves of consequence.

That change in direction was just what the sport needed, and suited Guilherme down to the ground – he won his fifth and sixth world titles back-to-back in 2001 and 2002, before Damian King stole his crown for the next two years, once more knocking him into second place. Those results meant that Guilherme had either been world champion or runner-up for 11 of the previous 12 years. "The hardest thing isn't winning once, it's winning the second time," he said. "You don't see many people accomplishing that feat, a lot of world champions come and go, but only for one time... they can't back it up the next year."

After returning to Rio following his fifth world title, he arrived at the airport clutching his trophy and wearing a

soccer shirt of his favourite club, Vasco da Gama. With the nation's press ready to greet him off the plane, newspaper images of him in the shirt were duly seen by his beloved club, which promptly invited him to meet the president. Off the back of a handshake the club agreed to sponsor Guilherme, who soon made appearances at the ground in front of 10,000 fans chanting his name. The decision for a big soccer club to sponsor a bodyboarder had a profound effect; it increased exposure and sparked a new wave of soccer clubs backing bodyboarders, and later athletes in jujitsu, judo and volleyball. "Soccer club sponsorship spread to other amateur sports like crazy," Guilherme said. "And it all started after I came back with that trophy... it kick-started a whole movement in Brazil."

In 2002 Guilherme sealed his place as one of Brazil's most successful international athletes with his sixth world title win. Although narrowly missing out on the title to Kingy at Pipeline the following year, he remained

Above: Relaxing between heats during the Pipe contest, circa 1996.
Far left: Tamega's performance at the 2011 IBA Arica Pro went down in history, capped off by a death roll onto draining exposed reef from a 10ft section. When things get hairy, Guilherme come alive.
Left: IBA Fronton Contest 2011.

*"I've always had my own unique style. It's not the most beautiful style in the world, but I've never copied anyone… and as long as it works for me, I don't give a shit."*

philosophical. "If God wanted him to win maybe it was because it would be better for the sport, and help take it to Australia or new regions," he said. "I've always felt blessed, for my protection and for the waves that come my way… but everything happens for a reason." In 2003 he also met personal trainer Danielle Batista, marrying her the following year, and going on to have two children, Kim and Kiron. Taking a break for 2007, he came back strongly in 2008 but was narrowly pipped to his elusive seventh world title by fellow Brazilian Uri Valadao.

Throughout Guilherme's career it has been his emphasis on power rather than style which has polarised opinion on the way he rides. As the Australian-led movement grew to focus on style and technical perfection, riders in countries such as Brazil, Chile and the Canary Islands have learned to boost with a Tamega-like hunger, backed with brute force and guts. "I've always had my own unique style," he says. "It's not the most

beautiful style in the world, but I've never copied anyone… and as long as it works for me, I don't give a shit."

Nonetheless, while style critics denounced his lack of crossed fins and perfect posture, there are few that doubt his commitment to charging, especially when conditions get heavy. From early on, his savage approach forced competitors to go beyond the barrel and look to smash through the lips of the biggest closeouts if they were to keep up. In giant surf this gave him the competitive edge both physically and mentally, as the other riders knew he would attack every section going, no matter how dangerous.

Despite this reputation of apparent fearlessness, Guilherme says he requires it to survive. "I do feel fear, but my excitement and enjoyment overrides it… you need fear to keep

your eyes open," he said. "The danger comes when you say you don't feel fear. For me I feel it most when I first paddle out in big surf, but after the first barrel it turns into the best feeling ever." It's a sensation he still craves today as he hunts for that seventh world title at 40 years of age, still on his original 'tear-drop' Wave Rebel, and still frothing with that insatiable desire to win.

For Guilherme, the fame he has received in his home country has been a positive pressure, which he has both thrived on and used to help carry him through 25 years of competitive bodyboarding. "If it was any other sport I'd be a millionaire by now," he says. "But for how small the sport is and the exposure it gets, I'm very grateful for the space I've had… I gave a lot of happiness to a lot of people."

# Andre Botha
## *The Superkid*

South Africa's Andre Botha is the youngest ever double world champion, claiming back-to-back world titles in 1998 and 1999 at just 17 and 18 years old, respectively. One of the sport's most naturally talented and truly fearless riders, he arrived on the North Shore as a skinny blond-haired grom at 15 and immediately made a name for himself at Pipeline, winning the Most Inspirational Award with a perfect 10. Over the following years he matured and proved himself in both big competitions and big conditions, which he loved to charge with a reckless abandon. In 2000 he survived the most spectacular wipeout in the sport's history at Teahupo'o during the famous Tahiti Skins competition, and went on to further his reputation in waves of consequence around the world. One of the sport's true characters, the unpredictable Dre has never been afraid of speaking his mind and carving his own line, no matter where it leads him.

**Andre Botha was born on 22 April 1981, in Cape Town, South Africa.** Speaking only Afrikaans until the age of 6, Andre was raised in Durban, a short drive from North Beach. After a happy time in primary school – where the headmaster would take pupils bodyboarding on a Friday afternoon – his education took a turn for the worse when he went on to a boys-only high school which engaged in corporal punishment. "That system was agony for me, I felt caged, it was worse than a jail," Andre said. "I did everything in my power to get out of that place." During this time Andre also developed a stammer when speaking English, which not only brought him embarrassment, but caused some teachers to believe he couldn't read properly.

Outside of school, 13-year-old Andre spent the majority of his time at North Beach, hanging around with a close-knit gang of local rebels, riders and outcasts. By now drinking and involving himself with the darker side of North Beach life, he was also drawn to the size and power of the swells that rolled in and detonated in heavy closeouts. "I earned my respect out there when it was big, like 8-10ft plus," he said. "Not to mention the paddle out was f--king hard when it was big, I couldn't even duckdive the big things, I had to swim out... the guys I hung out with got the most respect out there by taking off on the biggest closeouts, and I was doing the same thing, but I was five years younger than them."

As a slight 14-year-old, the smallest board Andre could find in Durban at this time was a 42" Morey Mach 7 – much too big for his diminutive frame. Flicking through an issue of *BIM (Bodyboard International Magazine)* one day he came across a Wave Rebel advertisement featuring Kainoa McGee, and with help from his mother, ordered a 37" model direct from California. Now on a board the right size for him, his riding took off.

By the age of 15 Andre had had enough of battling the corporal violence in school and convinced his mother he wanted to study by correspondence – learning at distance. Changing to correspondence not only allowed Andre to break away from the classroom he resented so much, but also to spend more time in the water. Involving himself early in the competition scene, he dominated the boys' division of the local Heatwave Bodyboarding Club contests and those held by the South African Bodyboarding Association (SABA). Having already been in contact with Wave Rebel when he ordered his small board the year before, in 1996 Andre competed at an event at Reunion Island which further impressed the company, enough to give him a couple of free extra boards to use that winter. At the end of the year Andre's parents paid for a ticket for him to visit Hawaii for six weeks over New Year, and he snatched the opportunity to make a name for himself in the biggest arena there was.

Sun-bleached blond and with a mouth full of braces, tiny Andre charged Pipeline seemingly without fear, and soon had everyone questioning who the South African supergrom was. On his new Wave Rebels his apparent self-belief shone brightly, from plumbing big Pipeline barrels and boosting aerials, down to the very boards themselves. "They had stamped them with Tamega's logo, so I rubbed his name out and wrote my name on there," Andre said. "He saw it one day at Pipe and got pissed off at me... I got all embarrassed and caught a wave in as quickly as I could!"

Yet away from his riding, Andre was very insecure; he was desperately shy and suffered an inferiority complex. Come the buzzer however and no one would have guessed. Entering the world championships in January, he scored a perfect 10 in his first heat of the competition, won the Most Inspirational Award at the post-event banquet and more importantly for his future, turned heads at Billabong. "I was used to massive closeouts at North Beach," Andre said, "... but Pipe was makeable, so in some ways it was easier." After Hawaii he returned home and continued with his correspondence schooling, but once Billabong tracked him down and offered him a contract and travel fund, the books were out of the window and the GOB World Tour beckoned.

Over the next year Andre took things much more seriously. Spending time at the Wave Rebel factory in California, he focused entirely on his bodyboarding, and with help from his mother who filmed sessions on video, started to see a trackable progression in his riding. However, despite this period of

*Waimea Shorey late 1990s.*

MIKE SEARLE

headway, Andre began to feel the Wave Rebel boards were hindering his potential. Wanting a different board but not wanting to lose a major sponsor, he contacted top shaper Nick 'Mez' Mesritz to get some custom boards made up that he could heat stamp himself with the Wave Rebel logo. With only three of the five events counting on the 1998 GOB World Tour, Andre missed the first event in Japan to be greeted with big conditions at Reunion Island for the second event. With most of the pack sitting deep, he spotted a better section and placed himself more off to one side, scooping into some solid ones to secure second place, before all eyes turned to Portugal. Andre finished third at Sintra, grabbed a fifth in Brazil and went to Pipeline in January needing to win the event with Tamega finishing no higher than fourth if he was to dethrone him and do the impossible.

Though held in small waves, Andre rose to the occasion and took the final from Bullet and Ben Holland – who crucially both placed ahead of Tamega – earning himself $4,500 and becoming the youngest ever world and Pipeline champion at just 17 years old. "I felt no pressure from other people or the media as I put enough pressure on myself," Andre said. "Because of my stammer, a lot of the time prior to heats I wanted to finish second so I wouldn't have to make a winner's speech... but in the heats I still gave it my all, and winning came to me." In South Africa, Andre's achievement made the front page of the Daily News under the headline 'Durban's New World Champ', and he was greeted by a big bus of Durban bodyboarders at the airport on his return.

In 1999 he arrived in Japan for the first stop of the new season heralded as a child prodigy. "I was treated like a superstar there," Andre said. "I was 18 and Japan was cool, they even had vending machines selling beer on the street! For that competition I rode this big, wide Toobs board someone gave me... if I saw a board I liked I always tried to get it off the person... so I took off the logo and stamped it Wave Rebel." It worked well in the smaller conditions, and Andre powered through the rounds to again face Tamega in the final. Not long after the hooter they both paddled for the same wave and clashed, resulting in Tamega being given an interference. "I basically won the final within the first five minutes because of that," Andre said. "I was paddling for the wave and he rode on top of me... he must have thought I would have backed down or something." After third places at both Reunion and Sintra he

headed back to Brazil hoping for at least a second to give him a good chance in Hawaii.

Andre successfully reached the final against – who else – Guilherme Tamega. "He wanted to beat me so badly, it was a personal vengeance out there," he said. "Not just for the previous year, but because I was just a kid, and he was a fully-grown man." Much to the delight of his cheering Vasco da Gama fans on the beach, Tamega trumped the young South African – who rode a Wave Rebel-stamped BZ Hubb – and Andre went to Pipeline needing to reach the final if he was to win his second world title. Again faced with small conditions, he focused on Backdoor and reached the semifinal, but trailed in third place with less than five minutes to go. "I was shitting myself, I couldn't believe I'd thrown away the world title," he said. "I needed a ridiculous score and was so nervous... I'd blown it." Then, in a twist of fate, the riders ahead of him tangled in an interference and Andre was through to the final by default – taking his second world title in as many years. "I was overwhelmed... but lots of people had underestimated me by thinking it was a one-time fluke the first time."

Over his two successful world title campaigns Andre rode a variety of different board brands, all sporting his homemade Wave Rebel stamp and sticker. While he didn't see a problem with it as he felt he was still representing the company, Wave Rebel didn't share his view and stopped paying him in 1999. "They broke the contract halfway through that year by refusing to pay me after I was ratted out by another team rider," Andre said. "But I would never have won the world titles if I'd had to ride their boards, they were horrendous. After they stopped paying me I saw lawyers about it as they owed me a lot of money, but hey, it is what it is, the industry is ruthless and I have an anger towards it. As world champion I should have been making a hell of a lot more money than I was... every company that I've been with has used me, taken advantage of me and lied to me."

At 17 Andre was earning $72,000 per year excluding prize money – $2,500 per month from Billabong, $2,500 per month from Wave Rebel, including his travel costs, and $1,000 per month from Island Style and Bluetorch. Now competing on the GOB World Tour, Andre began to base himself more in California between trips, where he stayed with friend Eddie Solomon. Andre had befriended Eddie during his first season on the North Shore through Manny Vargas, who had also introduced him to photographer Jeff Flindt. "If you know someone's filming, you are going to go bigger," he said. "You're going

*"After that wave I was over it, I wanted to get a massive one at Teahupo'o and I did… mission accomplished."*

to do dangerous manoeuvres which you might not otherwise have done."

In 2000 Andre travelled to Tahiti for the first time, arriving a month before the waiting period for the forthcoming Skins event. Riding a Mez board, his mind was set – all that mattered to him was to catch a monster at Teahupo'o. He made it through the first heat – but without having caught the huge one he was so desperate to catch – and was eliminated from his

second heat in the rain. Teahupo'o was angry; the skies were a slate grey and the swell irregular and dangerous. Disappointed he had not tamed the beast he had envisaged, Andre took advantage of the break in proceedings between the semi-final and final to paddle out for a freesurf to grab his moment. What happened next silenced the screaming boats in the channel and reverberated around the world.

"This huge lump came through and I said to Ben (Player) 'Are you going?' He said 'No way!' And that's where I made a mistake. At Teahupo'o it starts off small and gets bigger, but

my reaction was to paddle more for the shoulder than taking off deeper, so I paddled right into that big west bump. It was massive, and I let go of the board because I knew it was getting too crazy, that it would be more dangerous to land headfirst or on my stomach, so I tried to land feet first by letting go early." Andre slammed into the flats twisted after a freefall drop of 15 feet. "I knew as soon as I penetrated through the water I'd survived the wipeout, but I went down so deep that my leash was pulled straight above me and I was running out of air. I had to make the decision whether to get back up or stay down for another one, because if I surfaced at the wrong time I would have a massive one on my head. I waited but I couldn't hold my breath anymore so I climbed up the leash and thankfully there was nothing but whitewater everywhere… thank God there wasn't another one or I'd have been in just the wrong place. Compared to other waves and wipeouts I've had that was the biggest view of a lump of water I've ever seen… that thing was no joke."

Running on adrenaline throughout the rest of the day, it wasn't until that night that Andre began to feel a growing pain in his back. The next day Teahupo'o was pumping, and although he went back out on the boat to have a look, the soreness in his back meant he didn't get in the water at all for the next month. "It was worth it, that moment was glorious, when I popped up everyone went crazy cheering and it was only then I realised how big it had been," Andre said. "After that wave I was over it, I wanted to get a massive one at Teahupo'o and I did… mission accomplished."

Over the next couple of years Andre competed and travelled on the GOB Super Tour from his own savings as Billabong had slashed its support to $500 per month, before dropping him entirely. Emptying his bank account chasing the tour and partying throughout this period, Andre periodically rode for Unison Bodyboards before switching to Vortex Bodyboards in 2004. After failing to agree contract terms with Brian Peterson's company Andre felt severely let down and went off the rails, slipping into a wild three-month period of heavy drinking before quitting the sport and returning to South Africa. At home he was rushed to the hospital by his parents for blood tests and to see a psychiatrist. The blood tests showed Andre's cholesterol was through the roof. "The doctors told me if I had carried on drinking for another month I would have died," he said. "I was drinking 24 hours a day for months, barely eating, barely sleeping… it was a death wish." In a dark place, Andre started the slow recovery to get his life back on track by starting work at his family's guesthouse.

In 2005, after speaking with Mike Stewart and Eddie Solomon, Andre began to bodyboard again, now riding for Science with his own signature model. After his downward spiral the year before, Eddie told Andre this time he personally would deposit his cheques, and transfer limited funds each week to a new ATM card so he couldn't overspend or gamble it away. "Eddie took care of my finances as he didn't want me wasting money," Andre said of his addictive personality. "I had a lot of problems spending too much money too quickly… but hey, it comes and it goes." In the summer of 2007 Andre stayed in New York, where he drank heavily, partied hard and took cocaine each day, taking him to the edge and in some cases quite literally beyond it – one of his favourite rushes was to hang off buildings by one arm. "Drinking taught me a lot," he later said. "I wouldn't be the man I am today if I hadn't put myself through it."

After taking Eddie's advice, Andre signed a new two-year deal with Morey, earning $1,200 per month with a $6,000 travel fund. At the end of 2008 Andre jumped to Turbo bodyboards hoping it would provide the solid foundations he needed as a reformed professional rider. "Although I signed a two-year contract, Eddie told me Turbo had told him it would be for life," Andre said. However, after charging big waves, travelling, and competing intermittently on the IBA World Tour in 2009 and 2010, he and the company parted ways after failing to agree terms during the Hawaiian winter season of 2010/11. "I got hurt after that, I dedicated my life to this industry since I was 15," Andre said. "I thought it was alright, but after that it was the nail in the coffin for me in a way."

On September 17 2011, Andre was on a flight to Morocco when friend and sponsor Eddie Solomon passed away from an aggressive cancer he had been battling over the previous year. Although the pair had had their differences during this time, Andre misses him greatly: "He tried to take me to rehab, but I said I didn't need it… we found our way together. Eddie only wanted me to do better, we grew apart in certain ways and had conflicting agreements as far as greed goes, but it doesn't matter, he's closer to me now."

In January 2012 Andre married his girlfriend Tricia, who had a stabilising effect on his life. The couple first met in Hawaii in 2009. Exchanging art and poetry on subsequent trips to the North Shore, the pair got together in 2011 before travelling back to South Africa. Settling with Tricia has completely helped turn Andre's life around after his split with Turbo, and in 2012 the couple began working for Andre's father's renewable energy business in South Africa. While he has strayed from competition bodyboarding in recent years, Andre still loves to rush big waves and is most at home when things get heavy. "I always want the biggest waves, that's my driving force," he says. "I don't fear fear, there's nothing I want more, I enjoy it. The more scared you can make me the better I feel."

*"I always want the biggest waves, that's my driving force, I don't fear fear, there's nothing I want more, I enjoy it. The more scared you can make me the better I feel."*

Left: That wipeout, Tahiti Skins Event 2000, Teahupo'o.
Right: Canary Islands, December 2010.

JAMES FROST

# Oz Explosion

While the recession hit of the early 1990s decimated the careers of pro bodyboarders in the US, Australia, with its wave-soaked coastline and competitive spirit, took up the mantle as the epicentre of high performance bodyboarding.

**W**hile the United States' bodyboarding industry suffered in the recession of the early 1990s, the sport was taking off Down Under. After a steady increase in popularity throughout the 1980s, the run up to the millennium saw exponential growth in Australian bodyboarding, and it was only a matter of time before a solid national tour developed. Headed by the visionary Tom Wilson, professional bodyboarders flourished on the tour and set the sport on a path for greater things. Within the decade Australia boasted two new world champions and a plethora of the world's best riders, finest board brands, pre-eminent fashion labels and leading magazines.

Bodyboarding's popularity steadily grew in the 1970s in places such as Hawaii and California, and naturally all eyes were on the leading pioneers of Mike Stewart, Jack Lindholm, Pat Caldwell, JP Patterson, Daniel Kaimi and Phyllis Dameron. While Oahu's Sandy Beach had become the fulcrum of progression, it wasn't long before the first boards had made their way to Australian shores, and in 1981 Evan Penglis of New South Wales took out the first Australian national title.

Australia took to the sport gradually over the next few years, but its accessibility and functionality suited the nation's immense variety of waves, and lineups soon featured growing numbers of bodyboarders – particularly in the eastern states of New South Wales and Queensland. Before long, frothing groms were flocking to the prestigious annual national titles – held almost exclusively at the Sydney beaches of Long Reef, Manly, Maroubra, Dee Why and Tamarama – and in 1986 crowds were left awestruck by touring Hawaiian pros Mike Stewart, Pat Caldwell, Ben Severson and Tom Boyle.

By the late 1980s Australia's famed competitiveness had pushed riders from mellow beachies to gnarly reefs, in a steep learning curve of courage and machismo. South of Sydney, Cronulla's 'Skid Kids' dominated at the feared Shark Island, with riders Dave Ballard, Christian 'Rissole' Ricco, Doug Robson, Matt Percy, Mark Fordham, Brett Young, Warren 'Wazza' Feinbeer and later Adam 'Wingnut' Smith all charging its big, warping slabs and heralding a new buzzword for the sport Down Under – hardcore. In November 1989 *Riptide* magazine was launched, with Dave Ballard boosting an air at Suck Rock on the cover. The magazine became the go-to resource and successfully paved the way for future Aussie publications such as *Australian Bodyboarder*, and later the cultured *Movement* and *Le Boogie*.

By 1989 the Australian government had begun putting money into the promising sport, and led by national champions like Paul 'Barney' Barnard, Ross 'Hellman' Hawke and Steve 'Bullet' Mackenzie, bodyboarding was fast developing into a craze. Board sales went through the roof, and with strong board brands like Rheopaipo (formerly Paipo), Manta and Morey each generating profit to invest back into the sport, so the seeds of a self-sustaining industry were sown. Australian bodyboarding bucked the global recession of the early 1990s, and by 1993 had a king to call its own – Michael 'Eppo' Eppelstun, who took Australia's first world title at Pipeline and went on to be crowned Australian national champion in 1994. This year also saw the creation of a national tour by Western Australian bodyboarder and event director Tom Wilson, coalescing the country's disparate events and giving the sport a new professionalism and direction.

An avid bodyboarder and competition organiser, Tom had helped judge the 1989 Australian titles at Manly Beach, and went on to run state titles and stops on the Australian surfing tour until 1992. In early 1993 he began work for Morey in Sydney, and through Surfing Australia became the national development officer for surfing, longboarding and bodyboarding. With his experience of running the stand up circuit and its famous Bells event, Tom implemented the same principles for bodyboarding, using Surfing Australia's state offices and staff to make the new national tour a success. In addition Tom also set up the Mike Stewart Coaching Clinics at the end of 1993, making 17 tour stops in 21 days – the biggest coaching series Australia had ever seen.

By 1995 the tour had grown to nine events, with up to $5,000 prize money and nearly 100 riders signing up to compete at each contest. This was the beginning of the next

MIKE SEARLE

Above: Hailing from Avoca on Australia's central coast, Ben Holland launched his pro career by winning the Open Australian title in 1993. A fierce competitor, he was hotly tipped to be Australia's first world champion, but finished runner-up on the tour a frustrating three times. Eventually his hunger to ride empty reefs led him to launch a surf charter company in Tahiti.
Left: Steve Mackenzie always charged hard at Pipe.

BRIAN BIELMANN

CHRIS STROH

Above: To the outside world, Maroubra's Ross Hawke was the public face of Australian Bodyboarding in the late 1980s and early 1990s. Renowned for charging Shark Island and Pipeline, his sponsorship by Aussie board brand Manta helped the company build sales worldwide.

Left: Chaz McCall, a pommie from Brighton, was the first bodyboarder to surf Shark Island, in the late 1970s. After moving to the Cronulla Peninsula in 1978 he managed to get hold of one of the first Moreys in Australia and before long paddled it out to the mutant slab. He surfed the island alone for some time, but eventually inspired the likes of Doug Robson, Warren Feinbeer and Wingnut to tackle the place. It was photos of this crew charging at the spot that gave Australian bodyboarding a huge boost in the early 1990s.

Right: Nathan 'Nugget' Purcell built a reputation and career in bodyboarding in the 1990s through hard charging at Shark Island and on the North Shore. One of the sport's more zany characters, he invented the 'gorf' manoeuvre and, along with Dave Ballard and Doug Robson, was one of the infamous Skid Kids. He and Mark Fordham would go on to organise the Shark Island Challenge.

level for Australian bodyboarding. While big surf companies in the US were dropping riders and swiftly ending contracts, brands such as Rip Curl, Billabong and Quiksilver retained powerful teams and top names on their books Down Under. "We actually had activity and created media," Tom Wilson said of the surf brands' support. "We had something happening and they couldn't not acknowledge it."

Over the next few years the tour went from strength to strength and became a genuine rival for the Global Organisation of Bodyboarding (GOB) World Tour by holding events in conditions more favourable to high-performance bodyboarding. With a new wave of riders including Ben and Toby Player, Ryan Hardy, Sean Virtue, Damian King, Simon Thornton and Beau Day all raising the bar, it was Cronulla

local Andrew Lester who led the pack, winning the national tour back to back in 1998 and 1999, before going on to also claim the Mike Stewart Science Pipeline Pro on the 2000 GOB World Tour.

Within two years of *Riptide's* launch came Chris Stroh's highly successful video series, the Underground Tapes. First released in November 1991, the series focused on up-and-coming Australian riders ripping at home spots, and inspired thousands of young groms to take to the water on a bodyboard and get involved. From Eppo's gymnastics to Bullet's speed lines and Ben Player's technical perfection, it foretold the shifting balance of power in world bodyboarding. "Nothing was planned," Chris said. "Just hit and run and shoot everything that moved. It was all about the action rather

than quality." The series was soon playing in VHS machines across the country and inspired future bodyboard video projects including the No Friends and Tension series.

Chris White's Tension became another Australian institution. Blasting the latest generation of Aussie shredders into living rooms with insane footage and cheeky skits, the series helped build the careers of many top riders – including the likes of Dave Winchester – and paralleled the explosion of Australian talent onto the world scene. Several new Australian bodyboard clothing brands were launched around this time, namely Grand Flavour, Unite and Rejected, and bodyboarders across the nation lapped up the chance to wear labels unique to their sport – 'support your own' soon became a mantra.

The turn of the millennium also brought with it

Dave Ballard was easily Australia's leading dropknee rider in the 1990s. His ability to hit the lip and land his moves earned him more Riptide covers (including this shot) than anyone else, as well as long term sponsorship from Billabong.

big changes to both the national and world tours. After the success of Tom Wilson's groundbreaking Tahiti Skins Event 2000 at Teahupo'o and the epic 2001 Shark Island Challenge, the bodyboarding world had woken to the fact it needed a new tour to showcase bodyboarding on an international level, and Tom was ready for the challenge. In 2001 the GOB Super Tour got underway and lured many of the top riders from Australia – while the domestic tour suffered a little in this exodus, several of its finest exports were now on the way to bigger and better things. In 2003 Damian King was crowned world champion at Pipeline and backed it up with his second title the following year, before fellow Aussie rival Ben Player took his first world title in 2005 and his second two years later. The results capped off a remarkable Australian domination of the world tour, with no fewer than nine first and second-place finishes in the opening eight years of the 21st century.

The strength in leadership of the Australian national tour was clearly seen in the progression of its management into the world tour. In 1999 Tom Wilson began the shift away from running the Australian domestic tour to take over the GOB World Tour from veteran Bob Thomas. In his wake followed Aussies Steve Kirkman and Terry McKenna, who both repeated the process of first running the Australian national tour before moving to take control of the world tour from his predecessor. When Terry McKenna took over the world tour in 2007 he was joined by fellow Australian and head judge Craig Hadden, who also assumed the role of the International Bodyboard Association (IBA) International Technical Director.

A former competitor, Craig judged his first Australian titles in Manly in 1989 and head-judged myriad Australian, GOB and IBA events each year since, soon becoming recognised as the foremost bodyboarding judge in the world. In 2010 the IBA was taken over by IBA Pty Ltd, headed by Australian enthusiast and businessman Gregg Taylor. Alongside a revamped world tour and live streaming of events online, the move helped to develop the sport at a grass roots level by integrating eight IBA regions around the world, and creating a new structure which enabled progression from domestic tours to the Grand Slam Series of the world tour.

"The Australian tour is still seen as the premier regional tour," Craig Hadden says. "And with guys like Mitch Rawlins, Michael Novy, Jake Stone, Mark McCarthy, Sam Bennett, Andrew Lester, Lewy Finnegan, Ryan Hardy and Damian King all competing on it proves that. We see it as a real necessity that to compete on the world tour you have to come through your regional tour first, even the big wigs." It is this structure of development that has facilitated the progression of Australian talent in recent years, and successfully enabled the next generation to chase their aspirations. "If you provide opportunity it will grow," Tom Wilson says. "People will want to do it for the rest of their lives, and find a way to create a career out of it."

North Shore, 10 January 1997. Steve 'Bullet' Mackenzie becomes the second Australian to win the Morey Championships at Pipe, and what a way to win it – two massive and perfect swells pounded Pipe over three days, and the final day was as good as it gets.

16 PAGES OF BEACH BABES

AUSTRALIAN
Bodyboarder

Riptide
Australia's No.1 Bodyboard Mag

fiji's greatest pils

Newcastle's Hot Groms

Top: **Todd De Graaf** was one of the most talented and influential bodyboarders of the 1990s.
Above: **Toby Player** may have been overshadowed by his brother Ben, but he was always stylish and powerful. Dropping in at Pipe.
Right: Two thriving rival mags showed the strength of Australian bodyboarding in the 1990s.
Far right: **Adam 'Wingnut' Smith** was Australia's super grom of the late 1980s and 1990s. Sponsored by Manta from the age of 15, he built a nuts reputation for charging Shark Island.

# Ryan Hardy
## *The Natural*

Western Australia's Ryan Hardy is one of the most influential bodyboarders in the sport's history. Considered the greatest rider never to have won a world title, Ryan's ballsy commitment, textbook style and polished flair have made him one of the most respected and emulated riders in the game. In 2000 the then 20-year-old won the famous Tahiti Skins Event with a daring spin in the guts of a heavy Teahupo'o barrel – immediately going down in bodyboarding folklore as one of the greatest waves ever ridden. It is testament to Hardballs' dedication to making it look easy that many believe he is simply blessed with a natural gift on the bodyboard. The reality is for years he obsessively tweaked and polished each individual aspect of his riding to become the best in the world – a title his peers still readily bestow upon him.

**Ryan Hardy was born on 9 November 1979, with twin brother Brett.** Growing up three hours south of Perth near the small country town of Margaret River, the twins enjoyed playing in the bush and at the beach with their two older brothers, Gene and Josh. After being pushed into his first wave on a snapped foamie two years earlier, in 1988 Ryan went to Perth to pick up a secondhand Morey Mach 7-7, adding to the family's growing quiver of watercraft. By the following

Right: **Textbook North Shore invert, January 1998, Ryan's second season on the North Shore.**

year Ryan had added some grommet flippers, and with the advent of *Riptide* magazine that November had soon developed an interest in the gymnastic side of the sport, practising on the family's trampoline. "Once I was on the Mach 7-7 I saw a picture of Stewart doing a bottom turn with vacuum track rails and it just had this crazy appeal to me," he said. "I became fatally attracted to bodyboarding." For Ryan it wasn't just Mike Stewart, smooth turns and explosive aerials which so attracted him to bodyboarding, it uniquely also gave him room to develop an individual persona away from twin brother Brett, who had chosen surfing.

Above: **Winning the Tahiti Skins Event 2000.**
Right: **Driving through a pitching keg at the IBA Fronton contest in 2011.**

By 1990 Ryan had begun to draw inspiration from Cronulla's Skid Kids Ross Hawke, Bullet, Matt Percy, Nugget, Dave Ballard and Adam 'Wingnut' Smith, and in 1992 he attended his first competition in Perth – a Pro/Am featuring Bullet and Wingnut. "It was the first time I'd seen pros, and it was at that point my inspiration for it all just went through the roof," Ryan said. "Seeing them in real life and realising how genuinely world class they were, it was a huge buzz." It was also the first contest Ryan competed in, allowing him a public forum to unleash the competitiveness he had grown up with having a twin brother. "Every sport we had done we'd competed against each other, pushing ourselves," Ryan said of his relationship with Brett. "It was a natural thing for us to go into competitions, already having that mindset of concentration and focus to win... as twins it was pretty much born into us."

Aside from getting stuck into the Rivermouth at Margaret River, Ryan began surfing the beginner reefs of Huzzas and South Point further up the coast, developing a growing taste for WA's reef power. At 12 years old he first paddled out with his older brother Gene to the legendary Box; a heavy reef near Margs which unleashed big, spitting, square kegs and intensely thick lips. "I remember shitting myself, and being really scared of the sharks too," he said. "I didn't last long out there before paddling in." Ryan couldn't escape its mythical appeal though, and was soon lured back – it was a local break that looked like Hawaii and where only a toughened few would routinely tread. His older brother Gene was one such pioneer, regularly charging from deep in its jaws and paving the way for Ryan's future infatuation. At 14 Ryan felt he was finally ready, and on one 4-5ft day he paddled to the peak – without Gene – and caught two barrelling set waves. "The second one lipped me at the end and gave me a pretty good flogging, but I didn't hit the reef," he said. "I wasn't rattled too much by it, and from there I thought 'I could totally do this, it's on'."

In 1994 Ryan won the Cadets division of the WA state championship, picked up sponsorships with Manta and Billabong, and entered the junior division of the national titles the next year, finishing second. This result gave him a huge injection of confidence, boosted further by his first photo spread in *Australian Bodyboarder* the following year, an invert at Box. "It was the only day my mum had ever let me take off school," he said of the chance to bodyboard with his older brother Gene and renowned surf photographer Bill Morris. "It's the biggest buzz of anyone's life when they get their first photo in a mag and the path of being a professional opens up."

That path continued to open up for Ryan when he travelled to Hawaii over the 1996/97 season. "I approached it more as a spectator taking it all in, I was more interested in watching how things went down than getting in amongst it and doing crazy stuff for recognition," he said. "It was more of a trip of experience for me than of guts and glory." From an early age Ryan had learned to respect the power of big swells back home, and knew better than to push himself beyond his limits. "A

couple of times I didn't go out when it was massive as I didn't feel ready for it," he said. "I was just happy to observe, I felt I had more to gain by watching the Pipe comp and taking notes of how the best guys rode it rather than by competing in it."

Getting that initial North Shore experience under his belt and seeing the best bodyboarders in the world freesurf and compete at the Pipeline event coalesced Ryan's desire to make it as a professional rider, and he left Hawaii totally dedicated to his future in the sport. Having seen the majority of his contemporaries riding the Morey Mach 25 Fybercell that season, Ryan returned home and promptly left Manta – and his annual $2,000 travel fund – to get back on a Morey and progress at the rate he felt he had to be at. Graduating school at 17 and working occasionally at sponsor Wet Dreams Surf Accessories' factory making leashes, Ryan took the opportunity to surf his brains out during this period – twice a day every day – and saw an immense improvement in his riding.

By this point the Australian tour was as strong as it had ever been, and with riders such as Ben and Toby Player, Damian King, Simon Thornton, Andrew Lester and Beau Day all pushing the envelope, Ryan went through an exponential period of progress. Twin brother Brett also noticed a huge advancement in Ryan's riding during these years, even noticeable on a trip-by-trip basis through new moves, bigger aerials or cleaner lines. In 1997 Ryan travelled to the east coast for a month, and via Tim Jones was introduced to the guys at the Toobs factory (later becoming 4Play), who signed him up as a team rider. Back home in WA he started pushing himself in bigger surf – often by himself – and by the time he returned to Hawaii again he felt fitter, stronger and a greater part of the professional scene.

He now knew what to expect from the North Shore, how to handle the Hawaiian power, and by what means to make his presence felt at big Pipeline and Backdoor. That season Ryan's focus was clear to see; he surfed out of his skin and flew home from Hawaii in 1998 feeling his riding had moved up a notch in both its aggression and ability.

In the coming period he revelled in his increasing notoriety through international trips, magazine spreads and video sections. "All the buzz I had around my riding was just a reflection of how into my progression I was," he said.

*"Once I was on the Mach 7-7 I saw a picture of Stewart doing a bottom turn with vacuum track rails and it just had this crazy appeal to me," he said. "I became fatally attracted to bodyboarding."*

Right: **Flawless as ever, Hardy executing a
perfect air reverse at Off the Wall in 2006.**

"Bodyboarding was by far the most important thing in my life, and being a perfectionist it was the thing I loved the most... more than anything I wanted to become one of the best riders in the world." It had become a full-blown obsession for Ryan, and he would go to sleep each night thinking about how he could correct anything he'd done wrong in the surf that day. "Flawless style comes when you match the power of your riding to the power of the wave," he said. "It exists when you are at your most powerful, but also at your most relaxed." Midway through 1998 Billabong increased its backing, and with a new Toobs sponsorship he was able to become a full-time professional, earning a living solely from bodyboarding.

In May 2000 Ryan travelled to Tahiti for the upcoming Skins event with an ace card up his sleeve – he'd surfed Teahupo'o in big conditions the previous year. "It gave me such an advantage, because it's a wave that unless you've surfed big you cannot prepare for in any other way," he said. "It's such an extreme jump up from any other wave." For Ryan, this momentous contest was his time to be taken seriously at the highest level the sport had reached. Unlike many of his competitors, he had not had any big international victories in his career up to that point, and he entered the Tahitian competition more obsessively focused than he had even been before. "I had a goals page [in his journal] that I would read

every night before I went to bed, based around the mantra of 'Focus and achieve'," he said. "At the bottom I'd written 'You can do this Ryan, Tahiti Skins champion, 2000'." This focus was put to the test when halfway through the waiting period – when the surf had been consistently small and crowded – he was struck with the flu and bedridden for two days. For Ryan it seemed destined the event would either not be held, or if swell did arrive that he would be too ill to compete anyway.

Fortunately, Ryan dragged himself through the sickness and got better just in time for the last couple of days of the window, when event organiser Tom Wilson's hyped swell slammed into Tahiti with full force. For the opening heat on the first day conditions peaked at 8-10ft from the west, but by the second day a new swell bump had mangled into the action, resulting in bigger 12ft lumps coming through more from the south, giving riders a little more room for manoeuvre. "It was the gladiator day," Ryan said. "No one was in the water when we got out there, it was big, gnarly and the riders in the first heat of the day were thrown in like guinea pigs." Focused and determined, Ryan reached the final to face Mike Stewart, Guilherme Tamega and Alistair Taylor. After the semis the wind switched a little onshore, and he returned to the beach for an hour to dry off and recharge before the biggest heat of his life.

Once the wind eased everyone went back out, just in time

Overwhelmed and starstruck by his company in the final, Ryan immediately let all three paddle past him for initial priority. After catching an opening shoulder hop, he paddled back out with Ben Holland's words of encouragement running though his mind 'Don't let them snake you Ry, do it for Australia!' and found himself in a position to stroke into a west one swinging wide. Much to the Australian contingent's delight, he scooped in for a barrel and earned an 8.5, giving him some breathing room if he could back it up with another solid score. Sensing he had a chance, this time he powered back to the peak to get in position and 'wait for a bomb'. Letting a couple go by, a decent-sized set finally arrived with a good south angle onto the reef. After Tamega plunged into one and claimed it for his tally, all eyes flicked to Ryan on the next one, dropping and scooping into a long wall that looked like it might hold up. The following ten seconds went down in history.

"I could see it would be a runner, so I positioned myself where I would be pretty deep and get a good length of ride out of it," he said. "No one had snaked me so I took off, fairly smoothly due to its direction on the reef, and saw it growing with an even peeling barrel section ahead of me. I guess by instinct, and the charged up energy I had inside me, I instantly thought 'Right, spin in the pit,' so I put all my focus and ability into making it flat and smooth so I wouldn't catch a rail, to come out of it with full speed to keep going. I went into the spin and came out

*He paddled back out with Ben Holland's words of encouragement running though his mind 'Don't let them snake you Ry, do it for Australia!' and found himself in a position to stroke into a west one swinging wide. Much to the Australian contingent's delight, he scooped in for a barrel and earned an 8.5.*

to see a freesurfing Andre Botha take off on an ugly set wave which cruelly held him up in the lip and delivered one of the most punishing slams to the trough anyone had ever seen at Teahupo'o. "If he had got hurt I reckon it would have affected me going into the final," Ryan said. "I mean, it seemed unmakeable, but if you're as ballsy as Andre of course you're going to have a go. I had my heart in my throat waiting for him to come up, but once he surfaced and had a laugh about it in the channel we all relaxed... still, it was scary to think something like that could have come in during the final." By this stage however Ryan knew he had no time to be rattled by it – instead he saw the wipeout as valuable for seeing just how calculated and accurate he had to be in his takeoff.

smoothly with the board staying nice and flat on the water, legs up in the air crossed, and came out full speed, spreading them out as the barrel came over me. I could see a little chandelier down the line I had to push through to make the last section and it was then I could hear the channel erupting." Everyone – be them riders, photographers, videographers, organisers, water patrol, judges, locals, boatsmen or passing seagulls – had gone ballistic at what they'd just witnessed.

Ryan made it through the last section and into the safety of the channel to be greeted with a cacophony of hooting, screaming, shouting and cheering, and he paddled back to the boats to claim the wave and celebrate – there were ten minutes of the final remaining but to him it didn't matter, that wave

was as good as victory. As the clock ticked down, Stewart, Tamega and Taylor couldn't muster anything to rival Ryan's perfect ten point score, and with the Aussies counting down the last ten seconds, he was unanimously declared champion. "It felt like everything I'd done had built up to that point," Ryan said. "From then on, everywhere I went people wanted to talk to me, telling me how sick that spin was, it was like the whole world had seen it...winning that event on that wave seemed to leave a mark on everyone's minds, it has been what everyone has remembered me for."

Towards the end of 2000 Ryan received a phone call from

Damian King in the final. Alongside the Tahiti Skins Event title in 2000 it was the biggest win of his career and it kick-started a close world title race with Jeff Hubbard. However, by December the mental stress of the possible title was weighing heavily on Ryan's shoulders, and he was rapidly losing sleep. "It was huge, I couldn't stop thinking about it every day," he said. "I'd be in bed by 9pm but then wake up at midnight and be up for hours with loads of energy." Unbeknownst to him, he was suffering early signs of a manic episode of bi-polar disorder.

had happened, and she instantly recognised the symptoms as Ryan's twin brother Brett had suffered with the illness previously. As Ryan was on a surf trip in WA at the time, she visited him to have a chat and to get him admitted to the psychiatric ward of the Bunbury Regional Hospital. "She said to me, 'Ry, you know you're not well, we have to take you to hospital tomorrow', and although I felt everything going on in my mind was real and rational, I still trusted her," he said. "Because I had faith in what she was saying was right, I told her 'Okay, if you think so, mum, you take me in.'" As Ryan was

"I was thinking I was talking with spirits and had all these superpowers," he said. "I was euphoric, I called my wife on the Gold Coast and told her I was Jesus and telepathic."

Mike Stewart telling him he'd exiled himself from the Riptide Peer Poll and that Ryan had replaced him at the top of the list – something he had dreamed of achieving since being a grom. "I was shaking, it meant so much to me," he said. "It was the one thing I wanted more than anything, to get that title was the biggest stamp that I'd reached the level I was so desperate to aspire to." He went on to win it a further five times in the next six years.

By the late 1990s Ryan had shifted away from stock boards and had begun to play around with custom shapes, drawing in a more streamlined template which narrowed at the tail for increased speed and manoeuvrability. Riding for Toobs and working closely with shaper Todd Quigley, Ryan had soon got his teeth into every aspect of board design and manufacture, underpinning his rapid development throughout this period. Experimenting his way through 50 boards per year, things bordered on obsession for Ryan before the Hawaiian season in 2003. "I'd reached meltdown point with it all," he said. "I had Todd make me eight boards, perfect boards, and I was getting so fine-tuned into fractions of every single detail it got to the point I would only be feeling what was wrong with each board, not focusing on my riding. I became so over-analytical I virtually had a breakdown over it." He ended up not bringing any of the boards with him to Hawaii and writing Todd a letter of apology. The following year Ryan signed up with bodyboard accessory company Creatures of Leisure, and finally tied the knot with his girlfriend Leah, whom he had been dating for five years.

In 2006 Ryan won his first world tour event, the Shark Island Challenge, beating Jeff Hubbard, John Showell and

GSS Contest, Puerto Rico 2011.

Jeff Hubbard had won the world title race in January. By May 2007, Ryan's symptoms had worsened further. Now hardly sleeping at all and with boundless energy, Ryan became mentally delusional. "I was thinking I was talking with spirits and had all these superpowers," he said. "I was euphoric, I called my wife on the Gold Coast and told her I was Jesus and telepathic."

Straightaway Leah called Ryan's mother to explain what

now experiencing a full manic episode he remained elevated on an unnatural high, and it was not until his overactive mind had been brought under control with anti-psychotic medication that he was able to fully accept the fact he had bi-polar disorder and needed to start to deal with it.

Ryan's recovery continued throughout the rest of the year, and it was hard for him to realign himself and find happiness. "I got depressed for several months and had to figure out who

I really was," he said. "The world was crumbling down on me at that point... it was the lowest part of my life." Ryan received huge support from Leah and his family, and especially twin brother Brett, who was able to keep him focused on moving forward as he had been through it all before. The break also allowed Ryan to reflect on what he had achieved, and to put his situation into perspective. While he had chased so hard for the world title the previous year – almost to the point of self-destruction – his goal had always been to simply become one of the best, and he had accomplished that already.

SACHA SPECKER

Knowing he had fulfilled the goals he'd set out to achieve fundamentally helped relieve Ryan of the pressure of becoming world champion. He bodyboarded infrequently throughout the second half of 2007, but by January of 2008 felt able to return to Hawaii to compete in the Pipeline event and start to get his life back on track. "The year before I got sick the competitiveness and hunger to win was so consuming... it was like the animal was out of the cage for months at a time," he said. "Since I've

recovered and got better it's been easy to contain it, and only let it out come competition day."

By 2009 Ryan was back to surfing near his best, and in February defeated the field at Pipeline in perfect 4-6ft conditions. With successive high-scoring tube-to-roll and tube-to-backflip waves, Ryan beat Pierre Louis Costes, Guilherme Tamega and Dave Winchester to claim his first Pipeline title, a decade after first entering the prestigious event. Away from his successful return to international competition however, Ryan was eager to start testing himself in a heavier realm. During his break from the sport in 2007 he had analysed footage of Chad Jackson and Brad Hughes towing in at a crazy new WA slab called The Right, and was now keen to take on the beast, which he saw as simply a 'giant version of The Box'.

By April 2010 he felt he was ready, and with a big swell brewing, he drove through the early hours from Margaret River towards Albany. Arriving in the pre-dawn murk, he couldn't see a breaking wave from the beach but could just about make out the bombie's whitewater rumbling a kilometre distant. He took a deep breath and reached for his wetsuit. Jumping in at 6am, he had to first tackle the 10ft closeout shorebreak by himself in near darkness. "Getting through that was hectic and pretty scary," he said. "But once I'd started the paddle out beyond it I was shitting myself, it was so sharky." The next 40 minutes was the scariest paddle of Ryan's life, through salmon-rich waters at the prime shark-feeding time of the day – two weeks later a man was attacked by a great white on the same stretch of beach.

After a nervy while, Ryan could start to make out the biggest pits he'd ever seen on a reef booming and spitting into the channel, and by the time he arrived the sun still wasn't up. After he'd timed the sets and mapped the reef, Ryan paddled over to take off on a few shoulders. At this point WA's premier tow-team of Brad and Chad plus a few others arrived on jet skis, aware that Ryan had told them he was keen to give it a go, but

stunned to see this lonely figure already in the action. Lining himself up with a boil sitting just beyond the ledge, Ryan proceeded to edge deeper to the peak and position himself in the inch-perfect place to have half a chance of making the drop down the super thick, fast-moving chunks of ocean. Despite a number of successful tow-in sessions since it was discovered, it was the first time anyone had ever attempted the previously-

thought impossible: to paddle in at The Right.

"There were a few I pulled back on as there was just no way of getting down them. Timing the drop was so critical to not get thrown with the lip," Ryan said of the 12-16ft behemoths. "It was a real cat and mouse game out there. Losing your position in the lineup and getting caught inside could end your career." Over the course of the next few hours Ryan caught around 20 bombs, all from paddle-power, and despite having to duck through the top of a few, didn't once get caught inside. "It feels a step above Chopes," Ryan said. "The swell is moving faster and it seems to break from deeper water onto shallower water, I'd say size-for-size it's a lot more perfect and rideable than Chopes... that session at The Right was the pinnacle of my riding, it tested my fear, my balls and my ability to charge."

In 2008 the global financial crisis meant Billabong dropped Ryan from its team in favour of Mitch Rawlins, ending his $40,000 annual salary. However, now back on tour and riding for VS, Ryan was shortly picked up by Joel Taylor's Unite clothing label and Void wetsuits to fill the gap. After his son Oliver was born on 22 January 2011, Ryan's priorities naturally shifted further towards his earnings. "Without the money I wouldn't be able to travel or compete in comps to support my family," he said. "Above and beyond my passion and interest for bodyboarding, it comes down to the dollars and cents, for the wellbeing of my family."

Within three months he had won the IBA Box Pro in big and wild conditions, defeating Magno Oliveira in the final at the very spot that had shaped him as a bodyboarder. With friends, family and loved ones watching on, Ryan provided a clinic in how to surf his local break, boosting tweaked inverts out of Box's bowl and launching a big textbook cylindrical roll on a heavy one in the final to claim his most treasured career victory to date.

For Ryan, winning that elusive world title is still his ultimate goal, but the pressure to do so is now less than it has ever been. Ryan's hiatus in 2007 didn't just give him time to

"All I ever wanted was to be one of the best, and I feel I've achieved that dream... and that, to me, is my world title."

relieve the pressure he had put on himself to win the title, but to consider instead his original aspirations, and to appreciate the lifestyle he had created for himself. "It allowed me to reflect on what it was to be a professional bodyboarder," he says, pausing. "All I ever wanted was to be one of the best, and I feel I've achieved that dream... and that, to me, is my world title."

# Tahiti Skins Event 2000

PY 3860

Guilherme Tamega in the zone as the world's surf media look on.

As the world ushered in a new millennium, the sport of bodyboarding was in need of something big. The GOB World Tour was becoming stagnant, contest riders had become used to grovelling in poor conditions, others shunned competing altogether. The sport needed a shake up, something momentous, an event to showcase high performance bodyboarding in waves that the world would sit up and take notice of. For competition bodyboarding in the 21st century, the end of the road neared.

Fortunately, it was the road that ended a kilometre short of the heaviest wave in the world – Teahupo'o. In 1998 the surfing world was shown the competition potential of the break at the four-star Gotcha Tahiti Pro, and in June 1999 Tom Wilson – who ran the booming Australian bodyboarding tour and was the GOB's International Development Officer – started planning a bodyboarding spectacular at the spot. By the following year everything was set: the best riders in the world would face off against each other in some of the craziest waves ever ridden in a skins event that would redefine the sport. Sponsors signed dotted lines, $2,000 entrance fees were paid, plane tickets were booked, and everyone's focus shifted to a small slab of coral off Tahiti's far south. It was make or break time.

The majority of riders began arriving the week before the contest window to stay with scattered local families in the area. Before long, the Tahitian trials were underway to determine which two locals would make the event; Nicolas Richard – dubbed the Tahitian Mike Stewart – and Florent Moana went through in 4-6ft conditions. Expectation was high with predictions of a building swell running throughout

the week, but to match the occasion many of the riders were vocal in their eagerness to run it in 'huge and heavy or not at all'. As the days ticked by, Teahupo'o was offering good-sized fun conditions, but nothing more. There was a promising buzz, but nailing an accurate forecast was proving tough – in addition to the basic charts online, every swell source seemed to have a varying prediction on what, if anything, was brewing in the South Pacific. All anyone could do was wait.

In the meantime the match-ups were picked in a lucky dip from a cardboard box, with three men in each of the first round heats advancing into four-man quarter finals. Tension was high, and few riders showed up to watch the draw. With conditions still not big enough for the main event at 4-6ft, it was decided the women's final should kick off instead, and Stephanie Pettersen, Soraia Rocha, Karla Costa Taylor and Neymara Carvalho all took to the line-up with a certain trepidation. With a packed channel of pros looking on, they gradually fought their fears and in wobbly conditions began to push over the ledge one by one. Towards the end of the heat Bullet screamed Stephanie Pettersen into a set wave which locked her in deep and spat her out clean: "When I started bottom turning I just thought 'Oh my God I have to put everything into this' and turned as hard as possible... somehow I made it out," Stephanie said. "My whole body was shaking with adrenaline after that wave, just shaking." The crowd went nuts, and with reports of an increase in swell for the coming days, the amp and anxiety were building.

Unfortunately the swell wasn't. For six days conditions went flat, the contest window was extended, and return-leg plane tickets were rebooked left, right and centre. Contest organiser Tom Wilson was fretting. Everything was paid for and everyone had turned up, yet everywhere was flat. Another swell – supposedly a big one – was due, but people had grown

Half an hour later Ben Player, Kelly Hunt and Alex Kinimaka were paddling to the peak for the first heat. After a peace-sign opener by Ben Player, Kelly Hunt scooped into a bomb and got kegged out of his mind for a perfect 10. The channel erupted, it was on. Yet a short while later it wasn't. While Ryan Hardy and Mike Stewart paddled out for the second heat (minus Paul Roach who had dropped out with a staph infection) an onshore wind whipped up, and the pair were soon faced with chandeliering death pits. The event was called off for the day.

That night the mood was electric. The opening heat and Kelly Hunt's perfect 10 had seared on everyone's minds, but with the onshores set to continue and only one day left in the window, even he had bailed back to Hawaii convinced the final day would be a wash out. At first light the following morning it seemed he was right. Raining and laced with a 40-knot onshore, conditions were wild and even the ever-optimistic Tom Wilson started to have doubts. He'd been up at 4.30am and driven around the island scouting alternative locations, but all were onshore and suffering. Things were getting desperate.

In the meantime Mike Stewart had been out on a boat to check Teahupo'o, and to everyone's surprise returned at 7am yelling and waving his arms around. Tahitian water patrol legend Vetea 'Poto' David was standing next to Tom Wilson when he realised what Mike was shouting about – the palm trees were indicating the wind had switched offshore. "IT'S ON!" Tom screamed, and within an hour people were suited up, ceremonially blessed and on boats to bob out to the dark and angry lineup. "It was gnarly, and no-one was in the water," Ryan Hardy remembers, comparing the event to gladiatorial combat. "It was really big and dangerous," Ben Player said, "But worse was that it was super unpredictable... I was scared, no question." South African Alistair Taylor agreed: "It was flat between sets but when they came it was like a nuclear bomb

"I was scared, no question...It was flat between sets but when they came it was like a nuclear bomb going off...you could get killed in that stuff." – Alistair Taylor.

restless. Frenchman Nicolas Capdeville and Australian Tim Jones had given up and bailed home, and as remaining riders went to bed that night the mood was changing. Maybe the event just wasn't meant to be.

The next morning a familiar, deep vibration was rumbling the ground underfoot – Tom's mythical swell had arrived, and arrived in style. As the contest was given a ceremonial Tahitian blessing on the beach, 8-10ft chunks were booming across the reef and going inside-out with a fair bit of west in them.

going off... you could get killed in that stuff."

Under heavy, ominous clouds, the previous day's swell had been joined by another pulse from the south, mixing in some bigger lumps at 8-12ft, but also giving the riders a better angle on the reef to make the critical drop. Ryan beat Mike Stewart in the first heat, but the onshores returned as the second began and proceeded to swing with the rain throughout the day, making successive heats volatile and forbidding. "It was crazy in that funky wind, but everyone was pumped," said reigning

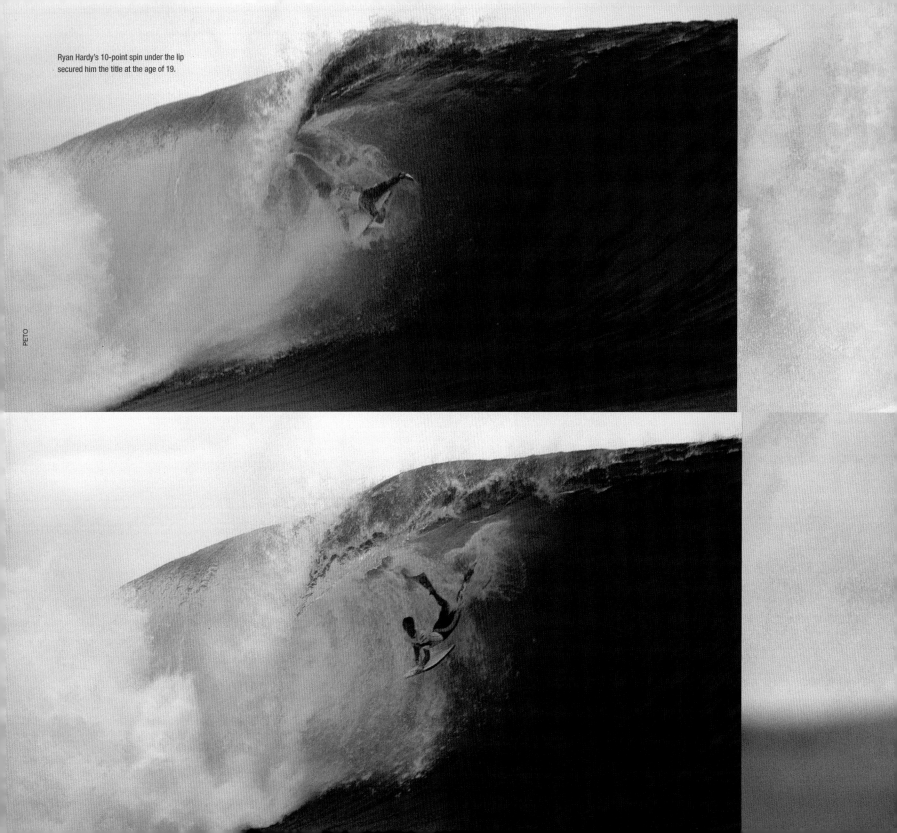

Ryan Hardy's 10-point spin under the lip
secured him the title at the age of 19.

PETO

world champion Andre Botha. "Just watching the action from the boats was mindblowing." Andre made it through his first heat but was knocked out in the next round, having not caught the monster he was so desperate for. Damian King, who had trained in the biggest pits of his life at Teahupo'o the year before, also got knocked out in the quarters. "There are animal waves out there," he said. "We were pushing it as far as we could, no one was pulling back." Anxious to prove himself, Tyson Williams snagged the biggest barrel of the event, pipping the diminutive Jeff Hubbard who also claimed a hefty one, spat out in a blast of Tahitian mist.

For many riders it was simply a battle of their nerve versus Teahupo'o. Teenager Mitch Rawlins couldn't quite bring himself to push over the mountainous ledges in his heat with Bullet, Simon Thornton wooed the crowd and cameras by scorpioning top-to-bottom in a spectacular free-fall, and Alistair Taylor decided to engage Plan B and hit the lip to launch on a couple. "It was the closest I've ever felt to being in war," Ben Player said of the final day. "It was a strange feeling, a mixture of pride and total fear." The atmosphere was heavy

> "It was the closest I've ever felt to being in war," Ben Player said of the final day. "It was a strange feeling, a mixture of pride and total fear."

and intense. Competitors battled with their own emotions as much as with their opponents: terror, exhilaration and relief flooded through their minds and bodies as they dropped into and rode their waves. The drama of it all was intensified by the blanket of grey rainclouds which hung over the warping chunks of Pacific Ocean.

Ryan Hardy and Mike Stewart knocked out Andrew Lester in the second semi and advanced through to face Guilherme Tamega and Alistair Taylor in the final. A one hour break was called to allow the riders some respite back on shore before the showdown. Andre Botha, so keen to have caught the biggest wave of the day, paddled out with a few others during the break with the sole intention of taking off on a monster and redeeming himself. Casually stroking into a jacking wall of water which was moving much too fast, he was too late making his drop and got hung out to dry on a lip so thick it had no back. Letting go of his board, he took a big breath and fell twisted into the trough as the wave detonated over him in an explosion of violence. Lumps were in throats as the crowd waited for him to reappear. As thoughts of a possible rescue were voiced in the channel, he finally broke the surface and

scratched out of the whitened impact zone like a scolded cat. His coiled Island Style leash was now dead straight, but he had survived the worst wipeout in living memory and got his moment in the spotlight.

As the final got underway Mike, Guilherme and Alistair powered to the peak past the 20-year-old Ryan, who initially seemed somewhat star-struck to have made it out there with them. Mike and Guilherme's decade-long rivalry still ran deep, and although they wanted nothing more than to outdo one another, they respected the gravitas of the situation more so. "It was not a heat to throw bad vibes or to be cocky," Guilherme said. "Snaking people could have been life threatening." After Hardy had an average opener he paddled back out into a wider one which offered him a big tube, snagging him an 8.5. Alistair caught a decent wave to start and backed it up with another, and by halfway through the heat there wasn't much in it between them. Guilherme knew two good waves wouldn't be enough, and with Mike struggling to find a rhythm, he would need to do something super heavy or different to boost his chances. Paddling into a dark, 10ft chunk of ocean, Guilherme dropped and pulled up under a crumbled section into the pit and above the foam ball to claim it into the channel. Hoots rained from the boats, but as he turned to paddle back out, the focus shifted to the next wave of the set – menacing, sucking, jacking, and with a little booger dropping down its face... Ryan Hardy.

Ryan had positioned himself in the perfect spot, and with full commitment he made the drop, scooped smoothly and set his line. He could see the section would run with a little room for manoeuvre. He pulled up high and realised quickly if he was going to do anything, now was the time. Concentrating on not catching a rail, he flicked into a forward spin with crossed legs, bounced high in the spit and whirled out of it with legs spread, air-dropping into a collapsing section, driving him through a second barrel and earning a perfect 10 on the judges' scorecards. The crowd went insane and he claimed it, paddled back to the boats and waited the last ten minutes of the final not wanting to watch it unfold.

As both Guilherme and Alistair had claimed two waves each they had no way of catching Hardy's total, meaning Mike was the only man who could topple him if he could find a big one. It never came, and with ten seconds left the Australian contingent were counting down Hardballs' remarkable victory.

The Tahiti contest was seminal and its impact enormous. It had set the benchmark for competition bodyboarding, countered critics and heralded the future of the sport's direction.

CHRIS POWER

# Damian King
### *The Multitasker*

The only prone and dropknee world champion, Port Macquarie's Damian King has effortlessly blended classic old school style with the new wave of explosive aerials. The biggest character on the tour, Kingy has one of the most idolised riding styles in the sport, combining power, finesse, and easily the best pocket surfing in the game. Known affectionately as 'The Joker', there is a lot more than meets the eye to the Breakwall legend, who has had his fair share of ups and downs over an extraordinary career that has inspired and influenced an entire generation.

**RVP** **24** **FUJI**

**24** **36 D 2**

The youngest of three children, **Damian King was born on 10 April, 1978, in the Victorian city of Melbourne**. His mother Sue had left Damian's father when she was pregnant with him, and moved to Port Macquarie on the Mid North Coast of New South Wales when he was four years old. Growing up in poor surroundings with his mother and siblings Sarah and Jason, Damian moved homes every six months for several years before his mother was able to find a state-funded house to settle in. A similar story for many broken families in Australia at the time, the difference for Damian was that his father was one of the richest men in Australia at the time.

Having made a fortune in the auto industry, every six weeks his father would fly Damian, Sarah and Jason from Port Macquarie to Melbourne in his private jet, escort them in Porsches and Jaguars, take them on helicopter rides around the city, and fit them out with a 'Melbourne wardrobe' of specially tailored clothing – which they would have to give back before returning home. "It was crazy," he said. "After leaving

Right: **Kingy's philosophy of not holding back paid dividends at the Tahiti Skins Event 2000.**
Below: **North Shore invert, 1997/98 season.**
Bottom: **Family snaps show early promise.**

slotted in a barrel. "I remember it vividly. I was just trying to get in, but I couldn't get out of it, and just started working it for all the speed it had," he said. "I got back to the beach and I was tripping out, I didn't even understand what it was, but I got addicted." Six months later – and now owning a pair of fins – Damian got hold of a Mach 7, and the beach became his de facto home. He soon developed a group of friends from the same Housing Commission area of the town and became a regular face in the lineup at top spot Breakwall.

Learning how to bodyboard in this pack helped Damian's approach to surfing in more ways than one. From a competition perspective, having riders such as new world champion Eppo, Peter and Vicki Gleeson, Luke Berhmann, Shane McEwan, the Murray brothers, Rick Bannister and Todd DeGraaf all surfing alongside him made a huge impact, including one of the top sponsored kids at the time, Mason Rose. At that stage Rose rode prone with a very technical style, and Damian looked to him for technique in the everyday waves Breakwall offered up. However, when things got bigger, older rider Simon Thornton was Damian's major influence in the group, who always dragged him out into the surf when things got gnarly. "I remember Thorto would never not go on a wave," he said. "And that way of thinking got instilled in me too, that no matter what, I would never pull back." By the time he was 16 years old, Damian had moved out of home and felt his bodyboarding was maturing too, as the technical and charge-hard elements he had worked on began to coincide.

Throughout his teens Damian had shunned the sponsorship chase, instead believing that if he was good enough, sponsors should approach him – not the other way around. For years he saw his friends compete, improve and get picked up by local companies, but still he refused to contact anyone. Finally, when he was 17, he won the Aleeda Bodybash in Queensland and was approached by Billabong, one of the biggest surf brands in the world. Suddenly he was thrust into the national limelight, constantly surfing with Eppo and trailed by top photographers, leading to the most magazine coverage he's ever had – even to this day. Indeed, Damian was getting so much coverage, fellow Port Macquarie rider and *Riptide* editor Rick Bannister started calling the magazine 'Kingtide'.

While Damian shot to the top in Australia performing in 4-5ft beachies, fellow up-and-comers Ben and Toby Player had gone to the ultimate proving ground, the North Shore, and charged hard – making quite a statement in the process. As Damian was seen as Ben Player's rival, the next year he knew he had to go there himself to avoid being pigeonholed as a beachbreak booger. "I felt a fair bit of pressure that first year as I felt lots of people back home wanted me to fail, and I was shitting myself," he said. "I was pretty young and I was petrified on the way there, I remember thinking I had a big job in front of me and I needed to dig deep." He did. Not backing down in any of the surf that hit the North Shore for those two months in 1996, he surfed some big days with only a handful of guys in the lineup, and after reaching the quarterfinals of the Pipeline comp, it was mission accomplished.

Back on home turf Damian started to do well on the

> "I remember Thorto would never not go on a wave, and that way of thinking got instilled in me too, that no matter what, I would never pull back."

Melbourne we'd have to go back to Port Macquarie and become rats again." Growing up with little to no money, Damian became streetwise from an early age, but having had these lavish experiences with extreme wealth, also became driven to succeed. "It was a real headf--k," he joked. "I should have been a serial killer not a bodyboarder."

One day when Damian was 12 he found a $10 'trendy bendy' bodyboard next to a river. A couple of weeks later he took it to the beach, and without fins, got stuck in a rip. Desperately trying to get back to land, he found himself picked up and

Australian tour, but with as many wins came losses, and he lacked any real consistency. "It was like banging my head against a wall really, it's been the story of my whole career," he said. "Constant peaks and troughs, but I've always found

North Shore lip glide, late 1990s.

though if I could just get through a trough there'd be a big high on the other side of it." Being plagued by a lack of steadiness even led him to consider leaving the sport on a few occasions, but he fought through the dark times with a dogged determination, a battle-hardened trait that has since become wholly characteristic of him. Damian thrived in high-quality surf, reflected in the fact he always felt he was tougher to beat in competitions when the waves were decent. "I just feel alive in good surf, I try to get amped in crappy conditions but when it's going off it's like a different feeling comes out of me," he said. "When it's pumping I just become an animal."

By the time he was 20, Damian had fallen out of love with Billabong as he felt they weren't investing enough back into bodyboarding, so in 1999 he took out a credit card and maxed it to $8,000 to start his own bodyboard clothing company on the quiet, Rejected. However, earning just enough to cover the $80 interest he owed each month, he needed more investment to really get the brand going. Getting his brother Jason and

fellow rider Brad Hughes to invest a further $7,000 each, the first selection of garments sold well in the summer of 2000 and the decision was made to start on a winter range for 2001.

During this time Australian tour manager Tom Wilson left the circuit to concentrate on helping to sow the seeds for the new GOB Super Tour and such era-defining competitions as the Tahiti Skins Event. By this stage, along with many of the new generation of Australian riders, Damian felt he'd almost graduated from the national tour and started to set his sights on challenging at an international level. After the bodyboard world went ballistic following the infamous Tahitian event, Damian went to the 2000 Shark Island Challenge on a high. In clean, 6-8ft conditions he finished second to event sponsor Mike Stewart, just missing out on what would have been the biggest win of his career. Determined to tame the Island, he returned to the event in 2001 stronger than ever, and as the largest swell in 30 years approached, the scene was set.

As crowds milled around the point at Cronulla and nervous

riders started waxing up, huge 8-12ft slabs were rearing and shearing their way through the lineup with guillotine lips. What no one knew at that point was that the night before – as Damian was settling down to sleep in his car – his brother had called with the news that Rejected's credit card was maxed, and the bill for the winter range was $10,000 over budget, at $22,000. With neither of them having any money, Damian was faced with the task of winning the $10,000 prize purse the following day to save his beloved company from bankruptcy. "I was shattered as I'd poured so much into it, and I think it was my first lesson ever in determination," he said. "I woke up that morning and it was massive, but there wasn't any doubt in my mind that I was going to win... I was 100 per cent going to win that competition, I didn't care who was there, which riders, which locals, it didn't matter." True to his word, with a fearless display of riding he took the event, placing ahead of Ryan Hardy, Sean Virtue and local hero Dave Ballard. It was marked in history as the best bodyboard contest ever held. The

He's not nicknamed The Joker for nothing. After announcing his retirement from professional bodyboarding in November 2012 he will be sorely missed.

"I remember when she took her last breaths I just walked out of the hospital and within five minutes promised myself there and then I would win the world title, or go and do something else with my life."

next day Damian was contacted by one of Australia's biggest multi-millionaire businessmen, Philip Brass, who had seen the photos of the competition in the newspaper and was so impressed he wanted to invest in the sport, and turn Rejected into a '$20 million company within three years'.

With Brass's investment, Rejected went big. From the $40,000 Damian and his brother had managed to turn over in the first year, it had taken $200,000 by the end of the following year, then $600,000, rising to $1.2 million by 2005. Despite this, it wasn't growing at the rate Brass had hoped, and he duly passed it back to Damian, Jason and the various other partners Rejected by then had. Unfortunately finding another big investor proved difficult, and being unable to handle half a million dollars of overdraft for stock, compounded by a few suspect business decisions towards the end, the company was liquidated.

In 2003, Damian's personal life came to a crashing halt as his mother Sue became ill with cancer. Returning to Melbourne in March, Damian slept on the hospital floor for three weeks and made sure he was with her to the very end, on 26 March. "I remember when she took her last breaths I just walked out of the hospital and within five minutes promised myself there and then I would win the world title, or go and do something else with my life," he said.

With that promise fresh in his mind, he began a gruelling regime of training, completely reworking his diet, and made sure he was in peak physical condition for the first competition of the new tour at Teahupo'o a month later. He duly took the event with a powerful performance in big conditions, and with a fourth place at Shark Island in June, he headed to Pipe at the beginning of 2004 needing to win the event to take the title. Multiple world champion Guilherme Tamega had run him close all year, winning at Shark Island, and as a result simply needed to finish higher than fourth. "I remember he didn't really talk to me and I could tell he hated me," Damian said. "It was tense, a proper battle." Four days before the competition at empty 12-15ft Haleiwa, Tamega arrived to see Damian checking the giant surf. Spotting him, Tamega put on his fins and paddled out, goading Damian to dare join him. Refusing to back down, Damian paddled out as well and the two exchanged huge waves and massive beatings without saying so much as a word to each other for the whole session. The rivalry couldn't have been closer.

Situated on opposite sides of the Pipeline draw, the two consistently made their heats and worked their way to the final – the ultimate showdown. Damian had spent a lot of time out at Pipeline that season. Remembering some advice

Mike Stewart had given him, he realised that with a south west wind Backdoor would hold open slightly more – a subtle strategy he put to work instantly in the final. Clicking his watch as he took off on his first wave, he scooped right into a Backdoor pit and scored a 9.5 within seconds of the hooter going. Backing it up with another high scorer, Damian felt confident he'd done enough to win, when a nasty duckdive paddling back out snapped his board. "After I'd swum in and got a spare board I paddled back out and Tamega tried to get an interference on me," he said. "But he was the one who ended up with the interference which pushed him to fourth... I'd won, it was like a fairytale, I was expecting Spielberg to pop out of the barrel and yell 'cut'."

After his mother died, Damian had divided her ashes into

> "I remember hearing the crowd cheering every time I fell off in that heat and I was devastated, and that spurred me on to get back out there and throw everything into it one last time," he said. Getting up backside, he threw a huge snap out of the bowl and another at the end of the wave for a 6.85.

thirds with his siblings, and split his share into thirds again. He spread one portion at a personal place where he used to go for picnics with her, another at home spot Breakwall, and the last third he carried around with him throughout his world championship winning season, finally putting them to rest at the back of the beach near the lifeguard tower at Pipeline, a spot where she would have been watching.

The following year Damian was determined to prove to himself that his first world title campaign wasn't a fluke. Having continued his hardcore training schedule, he secured a third at Shark Island in solid 4-6ft conditions, and another third at Sintra on the way to Maui's Honolua Bay, where the title would be decided. He would be battling Tamega once again. Up against Mitch Rawlins in the final – who had

virtually secured victory with two huge scores – Damian had little time left on the clock when he took off on a last-ditch effort and proceeded to land two air reverses on the one wave, gaining a perfect 10 point score and clinching his second world title. "Tamega came up to me afterwards and told me I was the luckiest person he'd ever seen in his life," Damian said. "He was rattled."

After his second world title Damian took a breather and relaxed from his intense training, married his long-term girlfriend Leona, welcomed the arrival of his new daughter Siena, and concentrated on sorting out his new house. Still on the IBA World Tour and ever the polymath, in 2011 he entered the dropknee tour to test that side of his game against the world's best. Competing in and winning various rated and non-rated events on the knee in Peru, Japan, Spain, Mexico and Reunion Island, he also finished second in Chile and Venezuela. Heading to Puerto Rico – having led all year – he only needed to get through his quarterfinal against Ardiel Jimenez to win the title, but was losing with 15 seconds of the heat remaining, needing a 6.8. "I remember hearing the crowd cheering every time I fell off in that heat and I was devastated, and that spurred me on to get back out there and throw everything into it one last time," he said. Getting up backside, he threw a huge snap out of the bowl and another at the end of the wave for a 6.85. "The feeling was as good as winning either of my prone world titles, I think because I was so close to losing it... I also kinda did it for the proners too, as I find many of the dropknee riders are arrogant," he said. "Dropknee is about having fun on a wave, nothing more, nothing less, and it says a lot that many of the DK riders haven't since congratulated me. Dave Hubbard hasn't even talked to me since I won, not that I care... maybe it's because I did it on a bat tail."

No matter how much he loves bodyboarding, for Damian nothing in the world comes close to his two-year-old daughter Siena, and he finds it extremely difficult to compete and be away from her, even for a week or two. For the last 18 months every cent he has won from competing – circa $10,000 – has been paid straight into a future bank account for Siena, which has helped him justify being away from her. "Bodyboarding is important, but she's growing up so quickly I don't want to miss a second," he said. "I've had a pretty good life, now I just want to make sure she does too." Indeed in November 2012 he announced his retirement from professional bodyboarding, citing a desire to spend more time with his family.

Right: **Celebrating the 2011 Dropknee World Championship in true Aussie style.**
Far right: **Slotted at the 2011 IBA Box Pro, Western Australia.**

BORN TO BOOGIE • 99

# The 2001 Shark Island Challenge

Island local Andrew Lester threads himself through Surge.

**I**f the Tahiti Skins Event 2000 opened the door to high-performance bodyboard competitions in waves of consequence, the 2001 Human Shark Island Challenge ripped it clean off its hinges. In perfect harmony, consistent offshore winds groomed the biggest swell the East Coast of Australia had seen in nearly 30 years. Roaring 8-12ft widow-makers unloaded across the fickle slab south of Sydney, and 24 elite riders suited up for what would become known as the heaviest bodyboard contest in history.

The Shark Island Challenge was in its fifth year. Devised by Mark Fordham and Nathan 'Nugget' Purcell in 1997 to grandstand elite bodyboarding in Australia, the notoriously heavy but fickle break hadn't yet bared its teeth in competition. This year was different: Shark Island was hungry, and the riders on the menu consisted of 10 locals, nine other Australians and five internationals – sans reigning champ Mike Stewart, who was awaiting the birth of his first child. It was Saturday, 7 July, the first day of New South Wales school holidays, and crowds swarmed the point, oohing and ahhing as some of the biggest waves ever witnessed as the shallow reef jacked and pitched in a churning exhibition of power and energy. What made this particular swell demand respect was not just its size, but its direction. Unlike the friendlier south swells, north and eastern ones wrap against the angle of the reef, deforming into multi-lipped mutants which pinch barrels and punch sections with steps and boils in a dangerous unpredictability. As local ripper Andrew Lester cheerily summed it up: "North Island is death Island."

As riders, organisers, spectators, media personnel and passing dog-walkers congregated at the point in the morning, the hyped and building ENE superswell was unleashing hell on low tide Island, closing out huge walls and booming onto

"When I first saw the swell that day I was like, 'Holy crap, you've got to be kidding me.' It was like eight feet Hawaiian and unloading at Surge…then I realised I was in the first heat and I thought 'Whoa, okay, I guess I better learn how to surf this place.'" -Spencer Skipper

Thousands lined the clifftops to witness the spectacle.

the exposed shelf. As the tide filled, all eyes were waiting for a makeable one to indicate there was half a chance of living out there. "You can't hold it in this, it's too north, people are going to get hurt," local Island legend Dave Ballard told contest organiser Mark Fordham. "You don't have to compete Bal," he answered. "But this is it." Such was the ferocity of the swell there weren't even defined sets, just giant corduroy lines marching in to unleash fury on those who dared don a rash vest. "I was quietly shitting myself," Ben Player said. "I didn't think they were going to run it."

"When I first saw the swell that day I was like, 'Holy crap, you've got to be kidding me'," Spencer Skipper said. "It was like eight feet Hawaiian and unloading at Surge… then I realised I was in the first heat and I thought 'Whoa, okay, I guess I better learn how to surf this place'." Until that point, the biggest he'd ever ridden Shark Island was a little over headhigh. Unbeknownst to all, Damian King woke that morning having slept in his car reeling from a phonecall that his new clothing label Rejected was $10,000 away from going under. With $10,000 up for grabs at the top of the podium, everything fell into place. "I didn't care how massive it was, I was winning that contest," he said. As he was putting on his rashie to paddle out for the first heat, Ballard casually informed him he would 'get smashed out there'.

Unrattled, Damian fed off the comment and immediately paddled out before the contest began, taking off on a big one and not making it. Fortunately, he avoided the bottom and popped up unharmed, instilling in him the confidence to push it further once the hooter sounded. He did. First wave of the heat he whipped a forward spin on takeoff and pulled in to one of the biggest kegs of the day. Thriving in the intense atmosphere, he proceeded to put on a clinic, charging virtually every good wave that came through and setting himself up as an early frontrunner. Things weren't going as well for Spencer – taking off too deeply on his first wave he was eaten alive. Ben Player had been paddling out and had a birds-eye view of the monster: "The wave just had like ten lips in it," he said. "It pretty much went completely dry. I was looking down from the top and just went 'F--k this'. I told myself if I made one wave I was lucky." From that point on Spencer was in a bad rhythm and not able to find any makeable ones for the rest of the heat. "Tahiti's heavy," he later said, "but after surfing the Island like this I'm sure it's heavier for its size... this place is f--kin' mean."

Huge, heavy, wide, fast, square, thick, pitching inside-out pits rifled across the reef as the tide grew, indiscriminately dishing out life-changing rides and life-altering wipeouts. Simon Thornton caught a bomb from the far side of White Rock, getting the crowd on its feet. For 20-year-old Andre Botha, the drops were as steep as his learning curve – he'd never surfed Shark Island before in his life. "It was scary as I didn't know the wave at all, I had no idea what was going on," he said. "The atmosphere was eerie, it was shallow, and people were on edge." It didn't stop him committing to anything he could paddle into though, making some barn-door barrels and taking some brutal beatings in the process, fortunately reef-free. He was learning to negotiate the Island's steps, ledges and boils in some of the biggest and heaviest conditions ever tackled.

Fellow South African Alistair Taylor had put in extra hours training prior to the event, and donning a white helmet, paddled out feeling confident and ready. On his opening wave he pulled into a 10ft closeout – somehow managing to pull through the back – but steadied the ship on his next one with a successful barrel. Coursing with adrenaline, a big line soon reared up and he didn't think twice. Fully committed, he made the drop but was quickly faced with a bouncing bottom turn and a boiled, square, multi-lipped wall of death. He knew the game was up immediately, and was violently tossed and cartwheeled over back-first into the reef, dislocating ligaments and pushing vertebrae out of alignment. "There was nothing I could do, it held me down with so much water pressure, then dragged and bounced me over the reef a few times," he said. "The first impact was the biggest, it was heavy... I was in a lot of pain for a while."

His effort graced the back page of the following day's Sydney Morning Herald. Back on land after the heat, Alistair temporarily lost the feeling in his legs and was rushed off to hospital, where the doctor bizarrely ended up punching his back to test for reaction. Sleeping with ice to reduce the swelling that night, the next morning he woke up stiffly, downed a double dose of painkillers and suited up to lock horns once more. "I shouldn't have even been thinking of competing," he said. "But the waves were just too good... I had to."

The second day saw a slight increase in swell size and a reversal of the heat order. This meant Damian, who had the edge overnight, was forced to sit and watch three hours of his opponents tearing Shark Island apart – with mixed successes. Alistair Taylor's second heat saw him take off on another ten-footer with the same reckless abandon he'd shown the previous day, but this time he aborted an attempted roll on Surge (the wave's critical end section) and went over the falls with the lip. "I thought I was definitely going to die," he said, remembering his plunge towards the drying reef. "Somehow I didn't hit the bottom though, it was amazing." The crowd, consisting of more than a hundred people in the channel and thousands more on the point, went insane. Meanwhile, in a buttock-clenching display of committed bodyboarding, Damian King's closest rivals Ryan Hardy and Andrew Lester had each put in a strong case for the title, and by the time his heat came he was awash with nerves. "I felt physically sick," Damian said. "All the pressure made me feel actually sick in the stomach." Paddling out for the final heat of the contest he composed himself and went about finishing the job he'd started the previous morning. Within half an hour he had chalked up three concrete scores, and had surely done enough.

During the 24-hour wait for the presentation, people reflected on just what they had witnessed off Cronulla Point for the previous two days. Not just the performances of the riders in contention, but also the waves themselves. It was some of the biggest Shark Island ever surfed and it had been tackled by the humble bodyboarding community. In front of a couple of hundred buzzing people at the presentation ceremony, Damian King's long wait was over. He took top honours, ahead of Ryan Hardy in second, and Sean Virtue in third. In the subsequent widespread media frenzy, the sport had cemented credibility; it changed the status quo, corrected misperceptions and importantly gave bodyboarders a huge source of pride. "Bodyboarding excels in waves like Shark Island," Spencer Skipper said. "That contest was the forefront of wave riding, there was no denying it."

*He made the drop but was quickly faced with a bouncing bottom turn and a boiled, square, multi-lipped wall of death. He knew the game was up immediately.*

# JØff Hubbard
## *The Aerialist*

Three-times world champion Jeff Hubbard took Eppo's aerial revolution of the early 1990s to new levels in the early 2000s, boosting higher and further than any of his contemporaries and attempting – and landing – moves previously thought impossible. One of the most explosive and entertaining riders to watch, Jeff's vision and courage in hitting the heaviest of sections has clocked him more air-time than any other rider and set the bar for what could be done off the lip. An original member of the No Friends movement, Jeff's unique style and dedicated approach to his art has inspired tens of thousands to hit the boost button and get creative.

**Born on 21 October, 1975, Jeffrey Dean Hubbard grew up the eldest of three brothers on the Lihue Sugar Plantation, Kauai.** The family enjoyed free housing as his father worked for the company, and at an early age Jeff and his younger brothers Mike and Dave played in the cane fields, built forts and learned to surf together at the nearby Kalapaki Bay on

Above: **Early shots from the family archive.**
Right: Hubb's aerial arsenal was well
developed by the time this shot was taken
on the North Shore in 1999.

Helping out with an IBA clinic in Mexico.

an old cat-scratched Morey 123. "I remember getting insane stomach rash from it due to the claw scratches on the deck," Jeff said. "And coupled with the crazy sunburn I was getting on my back, it wasn't too much fun." Regardless, Jeff put in the hours and got to know every left and right beachie peak and wedge reef out there, scooping into his first barrel in the shorebreak at nine years old.

By the age of 11 the family had moved from the plantation and Jeff began dedicating more time to the colourful new sport of bodyboarding, which had started to thrive in the islands. Learning with friends and neighbours his own age on his Haouli Reeves-inspired Scott board, Jeff soon began to go with local riders a few years older than him, and it was with them that he learned how to hit the lip and get air... the seed was sown. In the same year as the gospel-spreading Kauai Classic Team turned heads at the 1989 Gotcha Pro at Sandy Beach, Jeff left Kauai to go to boarding school on the Island of Hawaii, the same school his father had attended. "I hardly surfed for the

next four years at all," Jeff said. "We got off on the occasional weekend, but I didn't really give bodyboarding any more time until I left school at 18."

In his final year of school Jeff travelled to Tahiti and coincidently happened to share an overnight ferry ride with none other than Mike Stewart and new world champion Michael 'Eppo' Eppelstun. Eppo had exploded onto the North Shore in the winter of 1992 with a bold display of aerial boosts, and for six months had travelled with videographer Chris Stroh to film his video *Freakshow* — unleashing the game-changing air roll spin (ARS) and backflip in the process. An excited Jeff discussed the revolutionary new moves with Eppo that night, and realised the future of aerial bodyboarding hinged on them. "I always loved getting air, but when I spoke with him I started to realise what was possible," he said. "There were so many things Eppo did that I really admired, and I tried to utilise them and get exposure for creating new manoeuvres, just like him...I probably wouldn't have even attempted new

moves if it hadn't been for Eppo." The importance of that conversation stayed with Jeff, and within ten years he had created five technical moves the bodyboarding world had never seen before – the Hubb, Invert to Air Reverse, Air Hubb, Rewind and 720.

One day during his freshman year at the University of Hawaii, Jeff was surfing Rocky Point for the first time with a number of top professionals out. After catching a few good ones, Jeff's teen hero Hauoli Reeves paddled straight up to him and announced he wanted to hook him up with Morey, which was looking for new riders at the time. "He was so stoked on me, he wrote my number with wax on the bottom of his board," Jeff said. "I was absolutely thrilled... so I waited a week, but he never called." Undeterred, the conversation encouraged him enough to chance his luck with another company, and he tried Kauai Classic legend Harry Antipala at G&S in California. When he put down the phone he was a sponsored rider.

The Kauai Classic connection also extended to former

member Chris Burkhart, who Jeff had originally met in Kauai before moving to Oahu for college. In the following years Chris and his wife had also made the move to Oahu, and after meeting Jeff again took him under his wing – mentoring him for the contest scene, the North Shore and how to make it there as a bodyboarder. "He knew everyone, so all of a sudden I knew everyone," Jeff said. "He was hanging out with Kainoa, now I'm hanging out with Kainoa…I was really fortunate to have someone like Chris who did that for me, I met so many people through him."

During his second year in college Jeff's younger brother Mike had entered an amateur surfing competition on Oahu, and Jeff agreed to look after him if his parents would pay his own entrance fee to compete in the bodyboarding division of the contest too. Earning a solid finish wearing Viper fins, Jeff took a

Above: You don't get to be World Champion without getting angry with yourself when things aren't going to plan.
Left: Hubb's air reverse in the epic final of the 2011 Zicatela Pro, Puerto Escondido.

deep breath and called company owner Fred Simpson, who to his surprise agreed to sign him up on the spot. He now began competing during college as an amateur, but it wasn't until he was introduced to mutual friend Spencer Skipper that he realised he might be able to make a living as a professional bodyboarder.

Spencer was five months his junior but had already turned pro, rode for Morey and competed in Bud Tour events on the mainland. He surfed powerfully with a silky smooth style and linked his manoeuvres with effortless flow. "I surfed Diamond Head with him one day and he was just tearing it up," Jeff said. "I remember thinking, whoa, this guy's miles beyond my level… he's the real deal." The following year Spencer finished second behind Mike Stewart at the Pipeline championships, launching his career and earning him $4,000 in the process.

Watching Spencer come so close to winning such a prestigious event at just 19 years old gave Jeff a huge inspiration to better himself and step it up in the contest arena.

In 1995 he attended his first world tour competition in Japan, arranged by Toobs rider Chris Won. The experience was an eye-opener for Jeff, who consequently worked harder in the water, signed with Toobs himself, and started making finals on the Bud Tour. However, as his water time increased his classroom time diminished, and after a particularly fruitful early winter season on the North Shore, Jeff was handed an academic suspension for only producing a D in class. Now faced with a lack of parental funding, he was left with the choice of whether to head back to school, or instead get serious in pursuing his hobby as a career.

Deciding to go for it, he visited trade shows and started

peddling his contest results to look for a paying sponsor to be able to afford to continue living on Oahu. After some negotiation he struck up a pro deal with BZ at $1,100 per month, covering his rent, utilities and petrol – now he was set, and able to focus 100 per cent on his bodyboarding. In 1996 the new GOB World Tour was underway, and Jeff competed in a number of international locations including Reunion Island and Guadeloupe. "I turned 21 flying back from there," he said. "I had my first legal beer in First Class coming home from a contest as a professional bodyboarder, and I thought 'Hey, this is rad'." Nonetheless, the honeymoon bubble lasted only so long for Jeff, who had started to find the poor contest conditions disheartening. Despite a few event attendances in Japan and Pipeline over the next year, he made the controversial decision to quit the GOB World Tour and see where life took him.

What happened next launched his career and changed the sport of bodyboarding forever – the creation of No Friends. While the GOB was busy haemorrhaging pro riders in competition conditions not conducive to high-performance bodyboarding, Jeff and fellow disillusioned riders Ross McBride, Lanson Ronquilio, Paul Roach and Spencer Skipper decided to carve their own track. Paying Toobs videographer Brian 'Stoker' Stokes' airfares and giving him $200 a month, that year the gang spent their sponsors' travel budgets on hitting California, Hawaii, South Africa, Reunion Island and Indonesia to showcase on VHS the waves bodyboarding excelled in. The response was phenomenal, and with more than 10,000 copies of the video sold worldwide in the first year, Jeff's profile was set for superstardom. "It was the best thing I could have done, it was different, and I was able to make a name for myself," he said. "No Friends turned the sport around…instead of more coverage of Tamega winning in crappy 1ft beachbreaks on the GOB, it really appealed to the youth who had something

SACHA SPECKER

SACHA SPECKER

Victory celebration, 2012 IBA Pipeline Pro.

tangible to watch, it was a freesurf movement."

No Friends wasn't just a chance to travel with his buddies shooting footage, for Jeff it allowed him the professional room outside the pressures of competition point scorers to experiment and let his Eppo-inspired aerial side get freaky. "Travel was my job, but one of the ways to stand out was to do something new and different," he said. "I realised that to be noticed I had to focus on doing that to get exposure, it was helpful to me." He quickly created a trick move called the Hubb, effectively a forward spin-to-roll, then in 1999 invented a manoeuvre which has become much more popular in recent years, the invert-to-air reverse, or Inverse. First trying them during filming for the second No Friends video in 1998, he found it easier to convert a tweaked invert over into an air reverse than bringing his board back around under him before landing. "I remember surfing Off The Wall that winter and it was all I was doing," he said. "The Aussies tried to claim it as theirs in 2007 by hyping it up to belong to Dallas (Singer)… but I had to point out that I'd been doing them for a while." The following year Jeff also came to the conclusion the Hubb needed to be performed above the lip to look more explosive and functional, and quickly set about boosting the appropriately named Air Hubb, where both parts were completed before landing.

By 2000 Jeff was attempting the seemingly impossible: a 720. Having successfully landed one on Kauai that year, he went to the North Shore the winter of 2000/01 determined to land another on film if he could hit a heavy enough section.

The bodyboard world had no idea what he had in store, and one sunny day in early 2001 he went for it in front of the snapping lenses of the world's waiting media. Smacking a super thick double-up section at Pipe he boosted high and far, quickly winding off one air reverse and – much to the disbelief of everyone – attempting a second. He landed heavily just shy of the full second rotation and bounced off in the wash, but the bodyboard world went into meltdown. It was a ground-breaking move, resetting the benchmark of what was possible. "People were tripping out, it was so cool," he said. "Everyone was blown away, I think it broke a little mental barrier in people's minds, we realised there was so much more we could do." He attempted one more on the North Shore that season, but didn't land another on video until three years later for No Friends. Ever the creator, Jeff didn't stop there and in 2003 landed his fifth new move, the Rewind – essentially an air forward-to-front flip.

The No Friends years had started strongly, and by the time the second and third videos came out, the money had started coming in. Jeff and the crew had the backing of their sponsors and full-time jobs; travelling the world bodyboarding, filming

waves, and we were so desperate for these type of contests," he said. With the new Super Tour underway things were looking rosy, and by the beginning of February, 2003, Jeff's hard work was vindicated when he won the Rockstar Games Pipeline Pro, pocketing $6,000 in the process. It was his first time at the top of the Pipeline podium and something he would have to wait four more years to experience again, when he was crowned world champion.

Jeff's winning 2006 season started well, finishing fourth at big and wild Shark Island behind Australians Ryan Hardy, John Showell and Damian King. Buoyed by a solid result down under, his good form continued at pumping Arica in Chile with a victory, pipping Ryan in third. After a disappointing middle of the tour, especially at Sintra, Jeff looked to Maui to boost his campaign, in which he made the semis and finished fifth at chunky onshore Ledges. With everything set up for a Pipeline showdown, conditions blew up in the 6-8ft range with Jeff having to reach the final if Ryan made a heat, which he duly did. Now needing to step it up and relishing the pressure, Jeff advanced through his heats and not only made the final but took it out – ahead of Guilherme Tamega, Amaury Lavernhe and Andre Botha. "It was kind of a blur, I'd won the world title going into the final but I'd come out of the water not knowing what had happened with the comp as I couldn't hear the scores," Jeff said. "It pretty quickly became apparent I'd won though… it was a tough final and Guilherme was ripping, but I wanted to give it everything as you don't make a final at Pipe very often."

> *Smacking a super thick double-up section at Pipe he boosted high and far, quickly winding off one air reverse and – much to the disbelief of everyone – attempting a second. The bodyboard world went into meltdown.*

their exploits and boosting their respective profiles – the GOB World Tour was long forgotten. It was only after the Tahiti Skins Event 2000 and the 2001 Human Shark Island Challenge turned the world of competitive bodyboarding upside down that Jeff began to open up to the idea of regular competition again. "People were caught up in the buzz of competing in good

By 2009 the IBA's event order had shifted so Pipeline kicked off the tour, and Jeff started his second world title campaign poorly by not even reaching the semis. With that year's Shark Island Challenge then blacklisted, he and the rest of the international field went to South America with a point to prove. He won at Peru and finished third in Chile, before

TUNGSTEN

Hubb's first North Shore 720 attempt that blew people's minds in 2001.

heading to Europe to claim a second at Sopelana and victory at Sintra. The tour then headed to El Confital in the Canaries, where Jeff only needed to reach the quarter finals to eliminate the title hopes of Guilherme Tamega, Mike Stewart, Dave Winchester and Ryan Hardy. However, knocked out early by Ben Player, Jeff had to return the following day to watch the last three rounds to determine his fate. "Somehow they all lost in the quarter finals straight away and I had the title," he said. "The locals and Hugo Pinheiro just eliminated all of them... Hugo beat Mike, Diego Cabrera beat Guilherme and Guillermo Cobo beat Winnie... the previous night and that morning I had been stressing, but hey, it got a heck of lot brighter right around lunchtime."

It is not just his spectacular creativity in the air which has sparked comparison with Eppo, even Jeff's style above the lip rings true to the great innovator. While the modern day Australian style focuses on the technical critiques of symmetrically-crossed fins and inch-perfect front hand fingernail placement, Jeff always preferred Eppo's flamboyance of boosting frog-legged and twisting yoga shapes in the air. For Jeff, the technique argument is flawed. "I think the Australian style is only in vogue at the moment as the majority of bodyboarding's media now exists there," he says. "Back in the 1990s when it was all based in the States and No Friends was booming, that was the cool way to ride... now the magazines all hail from Down Under, it's no surprise that their style is peddled."

In December 2011, Jeff was a heat away from his third world title at crunching El Fronton. Watching on from a cliff top gantry, his hopes dissolved as Jared Houston couldn't knock an on-form Pierre Louis Costes, who progressed to win his first world title.

Fast-forward to December 2012 and Jeff was on the same cliff top, chewing the same fingernails. Having clawed his way back into title contention with a strong back half of the tour, Jeff could barely watch as his co-contender Dave Winchester battled through the rounds. The Australian needed to reach the final to win his first ever world title, and had scraped through his quarter to face Pierre Louis Costes in the semi. With the clock showing four minutes to go, Winchester was trailing but still had time to pull a rabbit out of a hat. Then the ocean went flat. In the middle of the jostling crowd on the headland, Jeff crouched down to escape the tension and pray the next few minutes away. With only a couple of desperate seconds until the hooter, Winnie quickly turned and dropped into a funnelling left to snag a deep tube on a mid-sized drainer. He popped out with the spit after the heat had ended, and the pair, the gantry, the world, had to wait an agonising ten seconds for the score to be announced. It dropped and wasn't enough. Jeff

shut his eyes, raised his hands and screamed – he had finally taken his third world title.

Seemingly a subscriber of the mantra 'age is just a number', Jeff is arguably surfing as well as he has ever done. The level he reached on his trip to Mexico in 2012 had people slack-jawed at what he was taking on. Huge, angry, cavernous, sandy, mountainous ramps were aggressively launched from on even the biggest of days, catapulting his diminutive frame over Puerto's terrifying trench and quarried explosions of whitewater. Now only a few years away from his forties, Jeff's fitness, flexibility, hunger and performance in the water regularly exceeds that of guys 15 years younger than him.

*"Back in the 1990s when it was all based in the States and No Friends was booming, that was the cool way to ride... now the magazines all hail from Down Under, it's no surprise that their style is peddled."*

"When I look back to heats I didn't win I do beat myself up to a certain extent, but generally I'm happy with the decisions I made... especially in heavy situations," he says with a shrug. "That's the way it is in this sport, we're not all dealt the same cards."

SACHA SPECKER

# No Friends
## *The birth of cool*

**The No Friends Corporation was founded in 1997 by a group of five young bodyboarders: Ross McBride, Paul Roach, Lanson Ronquilio, Jeff Hubbard and Spencer Skipper.** Disillusioned by the image of bodyboarding, which was still struggling to shrug off the "boogie boarding" tag of the 1980s, as well as grovelling contests in small surf, they set out to upset the old guard. Paul Roach is credited with coming up with the name: at the time US sitcom Friends was at the height of its popularity and the crew toyed with using "Friends" as their brandname. Hearing this, Roach, the most punk-ass member of the team, vetoed it on the grounds that he didn't want to be associated with such a wimpy mainstream TV show: "I don't have any f--king friends, lets call it No Friends," he said.

Starting with less than $9,000 in capital, they set up a makeshift office in 20-year-old Ross McBride's mom's garage in Camarillo, California, hired videographer Brian 'Stoker' Stokes and set out to film themselves and their mates freesurfing. Taking a cue from skate videos, Stoker cut the film to an eclectic soundtrack, a cover was designed and the vid was launched. Not really knowing what to expect, the crew was amazed when sales hit nearly 10,000 units in less than 12 months. More videos and DVDs followed at regular intervals, and with bodyboarders the world over buying into the No Friends definition of cool, plus five of the world's most talented bodyboarders as owners and team riders, they decided to expand and move into clothing.

By the mid 2000s No Friends was being sold in 21 countries worldwide. However, disillusionment soon set in. By the end of the decade Lanson had all but retired from bodyboarding, Roach couldn't make enough from bodyboarding to feed his family and had left to become a carpenter, and Stoker had moved on to other projects, unable to devote half his life to making bodyboarding movies. Despite this, No Friends certainly provided a template and inspiration for many rider-owned businesses which followed.

BRIAN BIELMANN

Paul Roach.

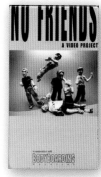

Ross McBride.

Spencer Skipper.

Lanson Ronquilio.

# Ben Player

## *The Perfectionist*

Twice-world champion Ben Player is not just one of bodyboarding's greatest riders, his dedication to the sport extends throughout its fashion and media industries too. Founder of game-changing Australian magazine *Movement* and premium boog clothing company Grand Flavour, he is one of bodyboarding's most influential figures. From his perfectionist style and tech riding to his cutting-edge threads and high quality publication, Ben has reinvested a great deal back into the sport which has seen him rise to the top and stay there for 15 years.

**Ben Player was born in Sydney on 23 August 1978, to English parents who emigrated to Australia in the early 1970s.** Growing up in the suburb of Leichhardt, it wasn't until his parents broke up when he was three that he had a chance to escape the landlocked inner west for the freedom of the Northern Beaches. At this point living separately from his father, a friend of his new stepfather offered the family the opportunity to stay at his vacant holiday home at Avalon, around 45 minutes north of the city. A beautiful area with good waves, Avalon was a multi-million dollar retreat from Sydney's hustle and bustle, and opened the door to a bodyboarding playground.

Despite growing up in a broken family, Ben got on well with his biological father, who enjoyed taking him and older brother Toby out on adventures in the bush and exposing them to the world. "He always used to throw us in at the deep end. One time he encouraged us to jump in this river somewhere in the wilderness with our bodyboards, and we got tangled around trees and almost drowned!" Ben recalls. "Another time we were sailing on a lake with him when the boat capsized in a lightning storm. We had to swim down and pull the mast out of the mud, and then some guys came and rescued us. These kind of things were just normal when we hung out with Dad." Whilst his adventurous side was nurtured by his father, it was Ben's stepfather, a surfer, who introduced the boys to the joys of the ocean, pushing them into their first waves.

As his parents worked hard to save and build their own house in the area, Ben and Toby faced a tough time in school as poor kids in a rich suburb. "I guess I was an outsider in the lower years in school, and Toby was like my best mate, we always used to hang out," he said. By the time he was 10 years old, Ben was hooked on bodyboarding and was spending much more time in the ocean. "I loved it straight away and would compete with the kids in my grade, so it was kind of payback time... they used to bully me on land, but in the water I could get my own back and show them."

As Ben progressed in bodyboarding throughout grades five and six, an interesting shift began to take place – he was no longer bullied, and even became cool in the eyes of his peers. At the age of 11 he wrote in his yearbook he wished to be a professional bodyboarder, and the summer before he entered high school he surfed every single day. At first learning on K-Mart specials, Ben and Toby progressed to an old board their neighbour wasn't using, and they even found a fibreglass board, which they kept attached using a leash made of shoelaces. Finally one Christmas Ben was given a Morey Mach 7-7, which he cherished and competed on for three years. It was this board that accompanied him at 6ft Outside Corner at Uluwatu on a motorcycle trip through Bali his father took him and Toby on when he was 14. "I remember I was so scared surfing those waves, but it was really great learning in those conditions, and experiencing a new place," Ben said. "I remember there was no road to Ulu's, we were on a dirt track, then we couldn't get home and had to hitchhike in this bus thing... he was always an adventurous guy, Dad."

Ben has always had a good relationship with his brother Toby, who both inspired him and made him realise a career could be made from bodyboarding if he wanted it hard enough. As he matured, it wasn't just Mike Stewart but the Cronulla riders Ross Hawke, Dave Ballard and the Skid Kids which impressed Ben the most, as they were charging Shark Island – one of the fiercest waves in the world. As he got more into bodyboarding, his parents decided he would need to improve at swimming, and signed him up to a local swim club. Here Ben dedicated himself to improving and competing, and was even in the running for the Australian Olympic team at one stage. "I'm really fortunate to have experienced all that swimming as it made me a really strong paddler," he said. "And to be able to surf waves like Pipeline you need to be just that." The swim training greatly increased Ben's competitiveness when bodyboarding, and it was at this point he started entering competitions at Avalon and the nearby Manly.

Ben's break came at 14 when he entered the National titles at Ballina in the Cadet division. Claiming second place,

Left: Ben tightens his finsavers for some Brazilian shorey fun.
Right: Flirting with the lens with a Bali backflip, 2012.

it led to him being sponsored by Morey and Quiksilver, and as he matured physically over the next couple of years his riding excelled. It was during this time Ben and his mates formed the Garage Gang, a small crew of boogers who began filming each other and surfing hard every morning. "It was amazing as it gave everyone the dedication and motivation to try harder," he said. Just as he was gaining a reputation for shredding at Avalon, a regional qualifier for the nationals was held at his home spot, and the writing was on the wall. He took the event, went to the Nationals at D'bah and won that too. The ensuing magazine exposure led to Quiksilver moving to get him on trips, and it was at this point he was introduced to videographer Chris Stroh, who was making the famed Underground Tapes series of bodyboard films. Stroh was looking to film younger up–and–coming riders, and it led to Ben getting sections on his videos and gaining exposure at a much greater rate.

For Ben, he stopped being a grommet and started his

was possible."

As Ben's riding developed so did his reputation for perfectionism. His consistency, repetition and dogged determination to constantly better himself were not just limited to the water either. "Most people get bored with the repetition of practice, but I don't," he said. "I get a real

By 2003 Ben's career was going well. He was earning good money through his sponsors and was getting solid results and coverage, when he was suddenly rocked as first Morey then Quiksilver pulled their sponsorship within a day of each other. "I had the rug pulled from under me," he said. "As a result I lost a bit of faith in bodyboarding as a career opportunity, and although I was quickly backed up by Mez at NMD, I was a little hesitant to give it all my time." Feeling let down by the industry, Ben decided it was the perfect time to start something up himself: a movement to cater for bodyboarders who didn't feel included in the younger scene supported by top magazine *Riptide*. "I started to wonder if bodyboarding wasn't cool anymore," he said. "I was in my mid-twenties, there wasn't any media focusing on my demographic, and I really wanted to feel I was a part of something." So, with a vision and an investment of $100,000 of his own money, the magazine *Movement* was born.

Speaking to his old friend and graphic design guru Murray Bell, Ben acquired the help of former *Riptide* editor Jethro Lyons and got to work. With little knowledge of publishing or set-up print costs and only estimations of returns from sales, it was a scary time for Ben, who had to pay for the second issue before he had any idea of how the first issue had sold. Regardless, he was comfortable with his decision: "I'd been lucky enough to have earned some money from Quiksilver, and it felt pretty cool to be able to re-invest all of that money back into the development of the sport," he said. With the first issue on the shelves in March 2004, bodyboarders lapped it up and it proved to be a game-changer, creating a new sense of community around the sport and broadly improving what consumers expected from a publisher. Although Ben never recouped his investment, it didn't bother him in the slightest. "From the get-go I wanted to produce a mag that would make a bodyboarder proud to pick it up and feel they could identify with it," he said. "It has done

*"Most people get bored with the repetition of practice, but I don't, I get a real sense of satisfaction from doing something over and over and accomplishing my goals."*

professional career when he travelled to Portugal to compete in a GOB event at 18 years of age. Losing to Tamega in the final, that second place cemented his mindset that he had what it took to make it. At 19 he was a regular on the national circuit, and regularly battled guys such as Andrew Lester, Ryan Hardy and Damian King. "That competitiveness and rivalry stayed with me and Kingy, and I would never have won my world titles if it wasn't for him," Ben said. "He showed me what

sense of satisfaction of doing something over and over and accomplishing my goals." Ben believes his lifelong love of computer games helped him develop the mindset to do the same levels again and again to increase his points. "As much as people say they're bad, I think computer games do teach you the art of perfection," he said "It applies in the water too, I'm never satisfied with almost nailing something, but if I'm making progress I'm happy with that."

In 2012 Ben ventured to the far north of Scotland to experience some cold water kegs.

just that, and I'm incredibly proud of every issue... I have an immense feeling of satisfaction every time I see it."

As *Movement* was in its infancy, the market opened up for Ben to explore his creative side in the avenue of a clothing company. Established companies No Friends and Rejected had sold well in Australia, but Ben felt the brands spun a negative connotation of bodyboarding being separate from surfing. Instead, he wanted to set up a 'sunshine brand' which promoted bodyboarding in a proud sense, and embraced the sport for what it was. Teaming up with riders Dave Winchester, Chad

Jackson and designer David Willcox, a year later Grand Flavour was created. For Ben, the company was never founded to make big profits – it was but a creative outlet to let his drawing and design side loose, whilst producing some clothing he would like to wear. "It was a really cool uprising in the Australian bodyboarding scene at the time, there was a real feeling that although we were small enough to have a close-knit family we were also big enough to have our own industry," he said. "We were truly beginning to become liberated." Releasing the first range of six tee-shirts, Grand Flavour went on to triple its

garment range, and become a leading global bodyboard brand – boasting singlets, shorts, shirts, fleeces, jackets, pants, headwear and accessories.

As his brands started to bear fruit on home soil, Ben's determination to progress in his riding on the tour led him to his first world title in 2005. "It was a total fluke," he joked. "No, I was a dark horse but managed to get there in the end, I felt like for once I was finally getting credit for the dedication I'd put into something for so long." After a string of second and third-place finishes throughout the tour, Ben

trailed Mitch Rawlins into the last event in second place: he needed the young gun to be knocked out first heat and for him to place higher than third in the final. Eventually finishing second, he won the tour, and was crowned the champion of the world, taking the title off old foe and reigning champion Damian King.

Despite his achievement and season-long consistency, there were negative murmurings in the bodyboard scene after he returned home that Ben was world champion without having won an event all year. "That really grated on me, I wasn't getting the respect in the community I felt I deserved," he said. Heading into 2007, and with those negative vibes still eating away at him, Ben was determined to prove himself and went hard in his training, practice, focus and planning. Shark Island was first up, and he took it out in style, following it straight up with another victory at Chile in 4-5ft conditions against Portuguese rider Manuel Centeno. This perfect start silenced his critics and almost ensured he had the tour wrapped up halfway through the season. After a couple of solid finishes in Portugal and Venezuela (where the judges somehow missed half of one of his waves) he went into the Canarian event just needing to finish higher than fifth. In glassy 3-footers he reached the final and was champion again. This time the victory was made more special by the fact his mother had flown over from Australia to watch him win. "That negativity after my first title was a massive reason why I tried so hard in 2007, to show them all," he said. This time, the message was clear – the best man had won.

For Ben, modern-day bodyboarding is split between technical competition riding and giant slab charging, with

> "I honestly hope one day I can reach a point where I'm finally satisfied, when I can say that's enough, and move on to do other things in my life."

both disciplines able to be traced back to contests like the Tahiti Skins Event 2000 and the 2001 Shark Island Challenge. Unlike many riders who shun competitions and the tour for cover photo glory on 20ft bombies in the middle of nowhere, he has instead focused on honing his riding in everyday waves, constantly striving for a higher level of excellence. His technical approach is second to none, with an emphasis on speed, and perfecting every move in his repertoire.

Ben believes the true test of a rider is how consistent they are in any given set of conditions – and consistency, he feels, is something more easily obtained with a love of repetition. "I get off on doing the same thing over and over again, I don't know what it is about my personality, but I get really excited by it and it helps my riding," he said. "It's like an OCD thing... I actually hope one day I get completely over it. I honestly hope one day I can reach a point where I'm finally satisfied, when I can say that's enough, and move on to do other things in my life."

Left: **Ben committing to the drop, Pipeline, 2012.**
Right: **Whipping a signature air forward, Java, 2012.**

# Boards

By **Sam Buckle**

*The original :* **This board is a first generation 'Tom Morey' production board that was on sale by mail order in the very early 1970s through *Surfer magazine*.** 45 inches (114 cm) long, these early boards were shaped by Tom in his backyard, glued together and finished off with tape. Selling them for $37 mail order, Tom was soon making so many that the glue was affecting his health, so he raised the price of the finished boards to $45 and started selling kits for $25, sending out the core, tape and skins. The customer supplied the glue. Despite this, demand for the finished boards soared. It wasn't until 1976 that Tom discovered that polyethylene could be heat welded together.

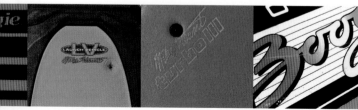

Rick Goddard Photo

Tony Prince Photo

# Winning riders insist on the Morey Boogie® edge!

### Exclusive Features...

If you like to surf and enjoy doing it well, the right board is your key to getting the most from every ride. The MOREY BOOGIE Pro•Line "Red Edge" has the extra stiffness needed for really aggressive riding styles and for pulling off difficult knee ride tricks. The red rail stiffener on each side plus thicker top and bottom skins keep the board's shape through high powered bottom turns and knee 360's. Takeoffs can be made easier and earlier too because of the board's higher flotation.

### Quality Construction...

Each MOREY BOOGIE board is carefully crafted in many separate steps using only the finest soft polyethylene foam core and skins available. When you insist on a genuine MOREY BOOGIE, you know you are buying the best.

Morey Boogie®

3229 Roymar Road
Oceanside, California 92054
(714) 439-0900

Keith Sasaki does it again! For the second year in a row Keith has won the SUNKIST / MOREY BOOGIE Pro•Am championships aboard a MOREY BOOGIE Pro•Line "Red Edge" board. The action photos above show him practicing some of the moves that helped him take the $1000 first prize back to Hawaii with him. Keith specializes in "drop-knee" and stand up rides and attacks each wave with a very aggressive yet graceful style. Congratulations Keith!

Watch for announcements on the 1982 SUNKIST/MOREY BOOGIE contest schedule. Start practicing now and be in the competition at next year's Pro•Am event.

SUNKIST is a registered trademark of Sunkist Growers, Inc., Sherman Oaks, CA

***Yellow Mach 7-7 :*** **The first slick-bottomed board, this was the second issue of the famous yellow board with black rails, now also featuring the orange bottom (the original had a poorer quality black slick).** Wet-gloved rails and a slick bottom combined to make a board that enabled the riders at the top of the sport to start performing at an unprecedented level. Possibly a bigger game changer than the Pro-line Red Edge that came out a few years previously, which had rail stiffeners but no slick. The board had a striped black nose logo, unlike the more familiar dayglo rainbow logo of newer models.

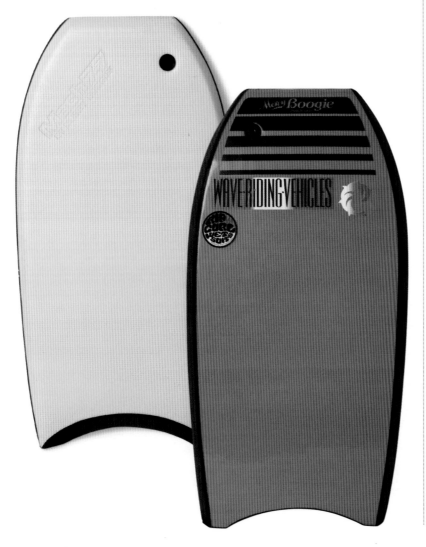

***Mach 7-SS :*** **The first board on the market to have a contoured deck, with its oversized thick rails and thumb grooves (designed for prone) it had the accidental result of producing a board that was great for dropknee.** The extra thickness through the nose created more flotation and the Mach 7-SS became the board of choice for dropknee riders like Jay Reale and Paul Roach.

Boards

**_Turbo Pro Comp III_** : **The third incarnation of the Mike Stewart Turbo board that, oddly, was available as a Turbo and a Morey model.** This was the first on the market to achieve the flex pattern of today's boards. Two layers of x-flex plus a Dow core created a recoil much better than the other stiffer boards of the same generation (which used rib-breaking Arcel). This was the board of choice of so many riders the world over, especially after Mike Stewart visited Australia on the trip made famous by the Tom Boyle video _Shock Island Down Under_. After this the board's performance could not be questioned.

**_Black Mach 7-7_** : **Arguably the first 'cool' bodyboard! Bodyboarders the world over saw a video or a picture of Mike Stewart riding this and they had to have one.** The refined template plus the X-flex core produced a design which is basically what we're all still riding, 20 years on. The only downside to the black colour was coming back to your car in summer to find a melted banana-shaped board that was never quite the same again.

**_Launch Vehicle_** : **The revolutionary features of the Launch Vehicle changed bodyboard design forever... but unfortunately this model was let down by poor manufacturing standards.** The groundbreaking design was first seen in US _Bodyboarder_ mag being ridden by Mike Stewart at Puerto Escondido, in a two-tone, black and white, and quite simply looked amazing. Talk of its futuristic features like the double-density deck with elbow contours, thumb grooves, and new bat tail created a buzz for what was the most eagerly anticipated board in our sport's history. It was only let down when it arrived by its lack of resemblance to the prototype! Problems in the manufacturing created a big thick abomination.

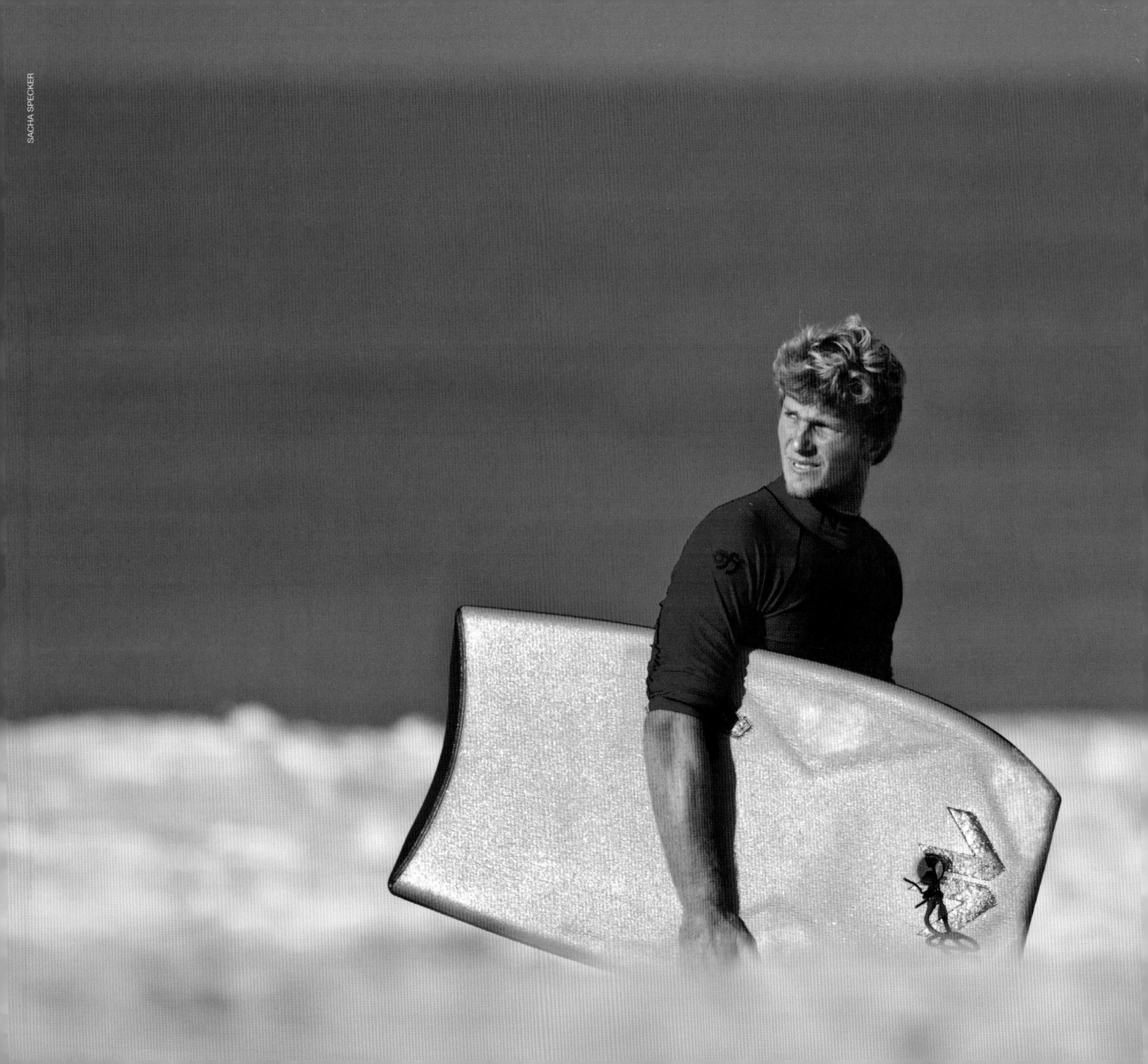

SACHA SPECKER

# Mitch Rawlins
## *The Inspiration*

**Mitch Rawlins was born on 13 December 1982, and grew up in Kiama, on Sydney's South Coast.** Relocating to the Gold Coast with his family at 13 years of age, Mitch soon made new friends and began to explore his local breaks, before joining the North Burleigh Bodyboard Club. Over the next couple of years he began competing in local, regional and Queensland Association of Bodyboarding (QAB) competitions, placing highly, and was soon picked up by Manta and Quiksilver. Striking up a healthy rivalry with fellow grom Jono Bruce, Mitch drew from Jono's technical approach and in 1998 won the national titles with a combined 29.5 out of a possible 30 for three waves – the highest combination of scores judge Craig Hadden had ever seen.

At 15 Mitch became sponsored by Billabong, made his first trip overseas to Hawaii and went ballistic. Among 200 other visiting Australian spongers he put on a cutting-edge display of bodyboarding, and impressed the entire North Shore including a certain Mike Stewart at Off The Wall, who would later take him under his wing and mentor him. Those six weeks kickstarted Mitch's career, and he enjoyed a large amount of worldwide exposure in the process. In 1998 he was in further talks with Mike, and by the following season had returned to Hawaii to stay with him and focus on increasing his power, cleaning up his lines and improving his style. This time the world's attention was focused on him, and the pressure of performing weighed more heavily on his shoulders than ever before, especially when conditions were big. Regardless, Mitch took it all in his stride, and over the coming years established himself as one of the biggest talents in the sport, gaining fans the world over.

In 2000 the 17-year-old prodigy competed at the Tahiti Skins Event at Teahupo'o, but faced with the biggest conditions he had ever seen, didn't catch a single wave. It was simply a step too far, and he came away rattled by the event. In the following years, however, he more than made up for it. At

Australian golden boy Mitch Rawlins burst onto the scene in the late 1990s as a freakishly talented grom, quickly mastering his art and tweaking his aerials to become one of the most exciting and inspiring riders of the modern era. From dominating competitions with a flawless style to freesurfing the heaviest of waves and more recently launching his own board company, 'Rocky' is one of the sport's most involved and influential figures.

CHRIS POWER

Mitch was still internationally unknown when he journeyed to the North Shore aged 15 in 1997. His riding that season launched his career.

Above: **By the early 2000s Mitch had dispelled any lingering doubts about his big wave riding ability by charging some seriously heavy waves. Check this Shipsterns mother.**
Left: Going huge in Western Australia in 2008.

*"I don't want to win multiple world titles like other riders. Just the one would be enough for me, to have been the best and most consistent bodyboarder for that year."*

20 he moved to Western Australia, conditioned himself, and towed into some of the biggest, heaviest, ugliest slabs ever surfed, rapidly developing a reputation for manning up when things got gnarly. By 2004 Mitch was surfing out of his skin, boosting higher than virtually everyone, and had his efforts rewarded by topping Riptide's Peer Poll, prizing it from Ryan Hardy's firm grasp. By the end of 2005 Mitch was in the running for a world title, and took out his first international event in Hawaii, at the Rockstar Games Honolua Bay Pro. Needing to back it up with another victory at Pipeline however, he was knocked out in the quarters and lost out in the world title race to fellow Australian Ben Player.

Mitch had performed with a style and fluidity that groms the world over aspired to. Shunning the contest scene, he became more known for his free surfing and big-wave charging, somehow straddling a line between underground shredder and global superstar, and in 2008 he once again topped Riptide's Peer Poll. The next few years saw Mitch's creative side flourish as he poured his heart and paycheques into producing his acclaimed video feature *Hiding From Comfort*. Shot almost entirely on 16mm by award-winning cinematographer Chris Bryan, it even included – at a cost of $7,000 per day to hire – some slow-motion footage from the 1,000-frames-per-second Phantom Cam. The film was a global success, adorned the covers of both *Riptide* and *ThreeSixty* bodyboard magazines on its release, and received widespread praise for both its quality and scope. "Shooting on 16mm is very testing sometimes," Mitch said. "We had sessions where up to 20 rolls of film would come back from the developers blank, so that was pretty hard to take... still, I've always felt the biggest challenges offer the

SACHA SPECKER

Left: Shortly after the Shipsterns session Mitch took big wave riding to a whole new level at this bombie in Western Australia.

biggest rewards."

In 2010 Mitch turned down a solid contract renewal with revered board sponsor VS to go it alone and create his own board company, Found. The realisation of a dream he had had for some time, Mitch set up the company to manufacture its boards on the Gold Coast, headed by respected shaper Jarrod Gibson. Having boards made in Australia allowed Mitch the research and development opportunity of surfing on a board in the morning, returning to the factory at lunch to make tweaks, and going back out on a redesigned model in the afternoon. The boards were performance-focused and technical, featuring new material compositions, flex properties and stringer placements. In August 2011 Found co-presented the IBA world tour event at Puerto Escondido, Mexico. In colossal 10-12ft conditions the contest went down as one of the greatest ever, and before long bodyboard retailers from as far afield as Europe were jumping to make room on their shelves for the label.

As the IBA began rehosting world tour events in waves of consequence, so Mitch's interest in competing grew once more, and in 2011 he requalified for the tour, riding for Found. In March 2012, he put on a masterclass in WA to win the IBA Box Pro, kickstarting his season and another hunt for his first world title – the elusive cap to an otherwise remarkable career. "I don't want to win multiple world titles like other riders," he said. "Just the one would be enough for me, to have been the best and most consistent bodyboarder for that year."

One of the sport's true visionaries, he has dedicated himself to bodyboarding in more ways than most, be it as a competitor, small wave shredder, style specialist, big wave hellman, peer poll darling, board manufacturer, video producer or custom shaper. Mitch's contribution to bodyboarding is vast, and his influence on the direction of the sport untold.

# IBA World Tour rebirth

**A**fter the Global Organisation of Bodyboarding (GOB) became the International Bodyboard Association (IBA) in 2004, it underwent a period of flux until Terry McKenna took the reins in **2007.** From just three contests a year it rapidly grew under his management and within two years had reached 17 tour events across men's, dropknee and women's divisions. In 2010 the rights to the world tours were signed to IBA Proprietary Limited (Pty Ltd), an investment company headed by businessman and bodyboard enthusiast Gregg Taylor. Separating into the Grand Slam Series (GSS) and Global Qualifying Series (GQS), an elite tour was created for the best riders to compete in the most extreme locations on the planet.

When Terry McKenna took over as General Manager of the IBA in 2007, he was faced with a problem. Whilst the sport had a growing worldwide popularity and its own burgeoning industry – especially in Australia – the world tour itself was not a tangible product with which to attract big sponsorship and gain forward momentum. Receiving conceptual documents initially drawn up by the visionary Tom Wilson and passed down through the organisation over the years, Terry expanded on their potential, developed details and formulated the proposal of an equity partnership. "After I first came along and looked at them I thought it would take forever to gain momentum," he said of working his way through the paper manuscripts. "I couldn't see any sponsors jumping on it until we had a product. No-one was going to bankroll a dream." Sure enough, after initial investment interest from the El Confital event organised in the Canary Islands in 2008, progress stalled during the following year, and by 2010 the IBA was forced to look elsewhere.

As Terry was getting to grips with what it took to run the world tour in 2007, the iconic Hawaiian bodyboard brand Turbo was relaunched by Gregg Taylor in Australia.

Opposite: **Alex Uranga** celebrates victory in the 2011 Reunion Pro.
Left: **Guilherme Tamega** works the crowd in Arica, Chile.
Below: **Amaury Lavernhe**, Reunion 2011.
Right: **Mitch Rawlins** powering back onto the top of the IBA podium with a consistent performance at Box, Western Australia, 2012.

Gregg had an investment background in high-risk venture capital with one of the world's leading asset management companies, Schroders, and by the Pipeline contest in February 2010 had begun talks with Terry over the equity partnership and future of the IBA World Tour. "It was clear that while the existing organisation had some very talented and passionate people, they lacked funding and were stuck in a vicious cycle of fighting for financial survival," Gregg said. "This led to short term decisions that had to be made but ultimately were limiting the growth potential of the sport." The pair were in contact throughout the following few months, and by the Sintra event in August 2010 Terry was in a position to present the joint proposal to the riders, who formed a majority vote in favour of the move. IBA Pty Ltd was given the green light, and the world tour had a new drive and direction.

The following year saw significant changes to the world tour at every level. Split into parallel GSS and GQS series, the former saw the top 24 riders in the world (plus wildcards and successful trialists) compete eight times a year at a selection of the best bodyboarding spots in the world. The latter operated an open format with the top eight riders at the end of the year being promoted to replace the season's least successful on the GSS tour. Alongside a shakeup in proceedings, the new tour also picked up broadcast sponsorship by international giant Red Bull and Fuel TV Australia, and appointed a full-scale media production team to document each event, providing live video, instant replays, short documentaries, highlight reels, rider interviews, professional photography and expert analysis as the season developed. In addition to the new unified world tours, the IBA also extended its reach to national tours to integrate eight IBA regions around the globe: IBA Australasia, European Tour Bodyboarding, IBA Latin America, Brazil National Tour, US Bodyboarding Association, IBA Hawaii, South African Bodyboard Association and the Japan Professional Bodyboarding Association.

One of the biggest and most important factors in the takeover was the live streaming of each event of the 2011 tour online. In an age of broadband internet, social media and live action, the new tour was primed and set to broadcast every thrill and spill of the season... and what a season it turned out to be. From Pipeline in February, the tour detonated at The Box, El Gringo, Puerto Escondido, Sintra, Reunion Island, Puerto Rico and went down to the wire in macking 10ft El Fronton in the Canary Islands. During the first event at Pipeline the live webcast attracted more than 300,000 unique viewers, with 500,000 visits and more than 1,000,000 page views. With an estimated six million bodyboarders in the world, the figures were revelatory. The 2012 IBA World Tour saw fresh sponsorship via YouTube, and by halfway through the season was registering 150,000 unique people a month visiting its website – in excess of double that figure during live events.

As the world recovers from the economic crisis, so the future looks bright for the commercial side of the sport, which has long been overlooked as an investable extreme sport in its own right. However, now supported by IBA Pty Ltd and with growing grassroots networks, a professional world tour and global media coverage, it's only a matter of time before expensive handshakes are made and corporate cheques are signed – allowing professional bodyboarders to finally earn what they're worth.

# Pierre
# Louis
# Costes

## *The Future*

SACHA SPECKER

Above: Who says chicks don't dig bodyboarders? Pierre and model girlfriend Rute Penedo.
Right: Perfectly timed air forward, Chile, 2012. Pierre's aerial assaults have become his trademark.

**With Pierre's father being a Moroccan swimming champion and his mother a competitive windsurfer, it's no surprise he took to the ocean with ease – it just took a while.** Born in the landlocked French town of Vichy on 25 January 1990, Pierre's initial chance of living next to the sea came when his family upped sticks to the picturesque town of Antibes, between Cannes and Nice. However, the French Mediterranean coast scores hardly any waves, and he had to wait until he was 8 years old to first experience open ocean swell when his family moved to Casablanca, Morocco.

Pierre took to the waves instantly, and after initially persevering with a piece of swimming pool foam, his parents bought him a 42" bat-tailed Mike Stewart Launch Vehicle for Christmas the following year. Despite being barely able to carry it, he learned quickly and even began using it as a stand-up surfboard. The year was 1999, Andre Botha had just won

his first world title and was on his way to another. Although magazines and videos were hard to come by in Morocco, Pierre had a treasured copy of the bodyboarding film 50/50. "I was just frothing on Tamega, Andre and Jeff," he said. "It just showed me what could be done on a bodyboard. It was miles beyond what I could do and I just wanted to be the same, it was crazy watching those guys."

Soon changing to prone, Pierre looked up to local ripper Adnane Benslimane and happily surfed with his mates at a beachie called Number 23, and the breaks around Dar Bouazza, a little hooked headland south of Casablanca. Yet it wasn't until Pierre met some travelling French professional riders and Franck Ehrhard of Hossegor Surf Club that he even considered sponsorship or entering proper competitions. "It was very encouraging hearing from them that I could have sponsors if I went back to France," Pierre said. "Franck told

me if I did that he was sure he would even be able to get me sponsorship from Rip Curl." Fortunately at 11 years old he did just that, relocating to Bayonne in southwest France with his family, close to the gaping barrels of Hossegor. The cogs turned and Ehrhard was right – he was quickly snapped up by Rip Curl, and has proven loyal ever since.

It was during his time in Bayonne that Pierre also took up skateboarding, especially during winter when it was too cold to surf. But his mother – wanting to steer him away from the skating crowd – soon ushered him back into the waves. After picking up Arabic at school in Morocco, Pierre worked hard to learn English, especially writing. In the water his talents soon exceeded those of friends his own age, so he started competing against riders who were much older than him. In 2002 – at just 12 years of age and with no-one knowing who he was – he entered the French Championships and won the under-14 division. Returning the following year he won it again at 13 and again the following year at 14, when he also entered the European Championship under-16 division with the French team, winning that too. This pattern of competing in junior divisions above his age was a consistent factor for him during his early teens, and one which drove him to work harder against peers with greater experience as he grew.

At 15 he made the life-changing decision to leave Europe and go on a roadtrip down the Australian east coast with friend and future world champion Amaury Lavernhe, who was 20 at the time. Eager to test their mettle against Australia's best, they entered the first stop on the tour at Duranbah, which Pierre won, beating reigning world champion Damian King in his first heat, and Michael Novy in the final. It was only after this victory Pierre started to realise he may have a future in competitive bodyboarding, and followed this up with a third

Left **Sucking in a deep breath before Pipe blows him out.**
Below: **PLC's first cover, early family snaps.**
Right: **IBA 2011, Puerto Rico.**

place at the second tour stop at Newcastle, NSW, eventually won by Andrew Lester. Pierre visited Australia three times in 2005, and opted to continue his schooling by correspondence, making room in his bag for books as well as boardies.

On his second trip in July, Pierre entered the trials for the Shark Island Challenge, where he was beaten by Michael Novy, eager to take revenge for his defeat earlier in the year. Following a jaunt to the Cook Islands at the end of 2005, Pierre then headed to Hawaii to try his luck at the Pipeline competition, still aged only 15. He got knocked out in the last round before the final 16, but not before a giant ARS attempt which got the crowds on the beach hooting. Despite not progressing he had made his mark, and by his 16th birthday his name was already a murmur around the North Shore.

When he got home, Pierre found he had seven new board contract offers to sift through – from industry leaders including NMD, Mike Stewart Science, BZ, and LMNOP. Choosing to go with Nick Mesritz's NMD, Pierre continued his assault on the European scene, winning the under-18 division in the French Championships and coming second in the under-16 division of the Europeans. By the time he was 17 the southern hemisphere season was a firm fixture in his calendar and he travelled to spend more time in Australia, honing his skills in punchy waves and starting to follow the IBA World Tour.

After getting knocked out of the Sintra event in 2007 he was given a huge boost by Nick Mesritz in the shape of his custom project VS. "I had just lost and was very disappointed when Imanol (Arrizabalaga) told me Mez wanted me in the team," he said. "I just couldn't believe it, he explained the project and I couldn't believe they had so much confidence and hope in me... obviously I said yes, it was a big push for my career for sure." The news boosted his spirits and spurred him on to finish third in the Arica competition in Chile, at that stage his most successful ever IBA event. "I was so happy with that result though I still felt I could have done better", he said. "But I finally felt ready for the whole world tour the next year."

And ready he was. In 2008 he stepped it up a gear, claiming third again at Arica, third in Brazil, second in Sintra and reaching a semifinal at Pipeline. By the El Confital event at Gran Canaria at the end of the season he found himself in contention for the world title, with Uri Valadao, Ben Player and Guilherme Tamega. Unfortunately, needing a second place finish, he bombed in his first heat. To make himself feel better after being pipped, he entered the junior and open divisions of the French Championships, winning them both.

The following year Pierre experienced his fair share of ups and downs. Starting off the season with a second place at the Pipeline comp, he visited Australia but suffered a heavy freesurf wipeout at the vicious reef Supers, twisting his knee ligaments. "It was the week before we had seven comps in a row", he said. "It was one of those crowded Nor'east days, it was at least 10ft and there were many jet skis around, it was hard to get a wave. Anyway a big one came, I took off too deep, got hit by the shockwave and then my leg hit the reef straight and I felt it twisting beneath me." Pierre battled on, managing to scrape a ninth in Chile and a fifth at Sintra, but after the European section of the tour he was out of contention for the rest of the year. However, his luck changed on arriving in Portugal for the Viana Pro, when he was invited out to dinner by Hugo Pinheiro and his partner – who had also invited her glamour model friend, Rute Penedo. The pair hit it off and steadily got to know one another during the rest of the year, a timely positive for Pierre, who struggled for results during the remainder of the tour.

Left: First-time world champion Pierre Louis Costes
salutes the crowds at Fronton, 2011
Right: Final day of the IBA 2011 Puerto Rico contest.

at small Sintra but secured another third at Reunion, meaning he had it all to do in Puerto Rico and the Canaries. "I had to win at Puerto Rico to be in contention, but Jeff also had to lose early, which is exactly what happened. It was destiny, a gift," he said. After Puerto Rico, Pierre travelled to the Azores to keep his competition momentum in full flow for the showdown in December. As the bodyboard world's focus moved to El Fronton for the final event of the 2011 tour, Pierre took the chance to arrive early and compete at the ISA World Games for France – gaining him some valuable competition practise at the fearsome slab. "Fronton can change a lot and is hard to surf sometimes," he said. "So I had the chance to surf it in four-man heats in some very different conditions." Pierre was unstoppable and took the title of ISA World Bodyboard Champion, the biggest win of his career.

Fast forward a couple of weeks and he found himself up against South African Jared Houston in the quarter final of the last event of the 2011 IBA World Tour. If he won the heat, he would be crowned world champion for the second time in two

> "In my mind people are a little bit bored with the moves today, everyone loves to see innovation. Creativity should be rewarded as long as it is aesthetic and functional."

After visiting Hawaii together in 2010 the pair were faced with a four-month separation as a reinvigorated Pierre got his teeth into the new tour, desperate to make up for the year before. "We didn't break up, but it was really hard to have a relationship when you are away for so long, after those four months apart we decided to get more serious... the key point was when I decided to move to Portugal." The relocation meant Pierre was able to spend more time with his newfound love between tour stops, and enabled him to train in some of the best and biggest waves the North Atlantic could serve up. It paid dividends. He pushed hard during the 2010 season, impressed in some solid conditions – performing the biggest competition backflip ever seen in Peru – but was again just beaten to the title, this time by his old friend Amaury Lavernhe. "I was happy for seeing my friend win and it was hugely inspiring for me," he said. "But it made me hungry."

It was a tough pill to swallow for Pierre, but he dug deep

and believed he now had what it took to take the title in 2011. "I had to remind myself it is a marathon, not a sprint," Pierre said after a slow start, which saw Jeff Hubbard, Ryan Hardy and Guilherme Tamega take wins at Pipeline, The Box and Arica, knocking him out of the top ten in the process. Pierre's boyhood idols from his old 50/50 tape were now his strongest competitors. "Tamega and Hubb are the hardest to have in any heat," he said. "They've been there for a while now and just know how to surf every condition. There are a lot of good riders of course, but those are the toughest guys to beat." By event four in Mexico the pressure was starting to increase for a good result, and as the swell built on the final day, Pierre felt he had to silence critics who had commended his technical riding, but not seen him charge hard in the big stuff. Sucking it up, he did just that, finishing third and gaining some crucial points to make things fall together in the latter half of the season.

Pierre followed success in Mexico with a poor performance

weeks. If he lost, it would be tour leader Jeff Hubbard collecting his third world title instead.

In a blustery wind, big, ugly waves roared in and wrapped onto Fronton's shelf, producing thick blue caverns. Hubbard, already knocked out and watching on from the grandstand, was biting his nails as he saw Houston time and time again drop into gaping pits but fail to come out. With just a few minutes left, Pierre's narrow lead was solidified with a drop, scoop and deep right barrel for a 9-point clincher, and the crowd went insane. Pulling off onto the shoulder, he paddled back out, sat on his board and waited for the hooter. As it sounded, and with his family, friends and Rute screaming with joy, he raised his arms in salute to the grandstand and the captivated global audience streaming the event online. He was crowned IBA World Champion – his dream had come true, at just 21 years of age.

Becoming world champion so early released a fair amount

of pressure from Pierre's shoulders, but simultaneously gave him a taste he now craves. "Once I set my mind to something, I work very hard to achieve what I want," he said, also admitting he can sometimes be too hard on himself: "Although I am a perfectionist, and it is very hard to be satisfied with myself a lot of the time." He cedes this is also a trait in his personal life away from bodyboarding, a common quality of many top riders.

Fortunately, his rise to the upper echelons of the international scene has coincided perfectly with changing heat formats, redesigned to reward creativity in competitions. This chance to bring his freesurf flair into non-elimination rounds has excited Pierre, who believes new moves shouldn't be shunned in heats. "In my mind people are a little bit bored with the moves today, everyone loves to see innovation," he says. "Creativity should be rewarded as long as it is aesthetic and functional." There is no doubt in Pierre's mind however that his strongest competition in the future will come from Australia. "It is ridiculous how much young talent is coming out of Oz," he says. "Their style of riding has had a major influence on me and many other riders all over the world."

Despite Pierre's remarkable success, growing marketability and multiple titles, his happiness is heavily dependent on the ocean, and he has realised his mindset can swing strongly if it isn't playing ball. "It is my biggest weakness, I just need good waves," he says. "It is an addiction... my mood depends on the ocean."

Fronton launch, 2011.

Portrait of a pro who loves his life. Sintra, Portugal 2012.

# index

Lanson Ronquilio, West Side Oahu mid 1990s.